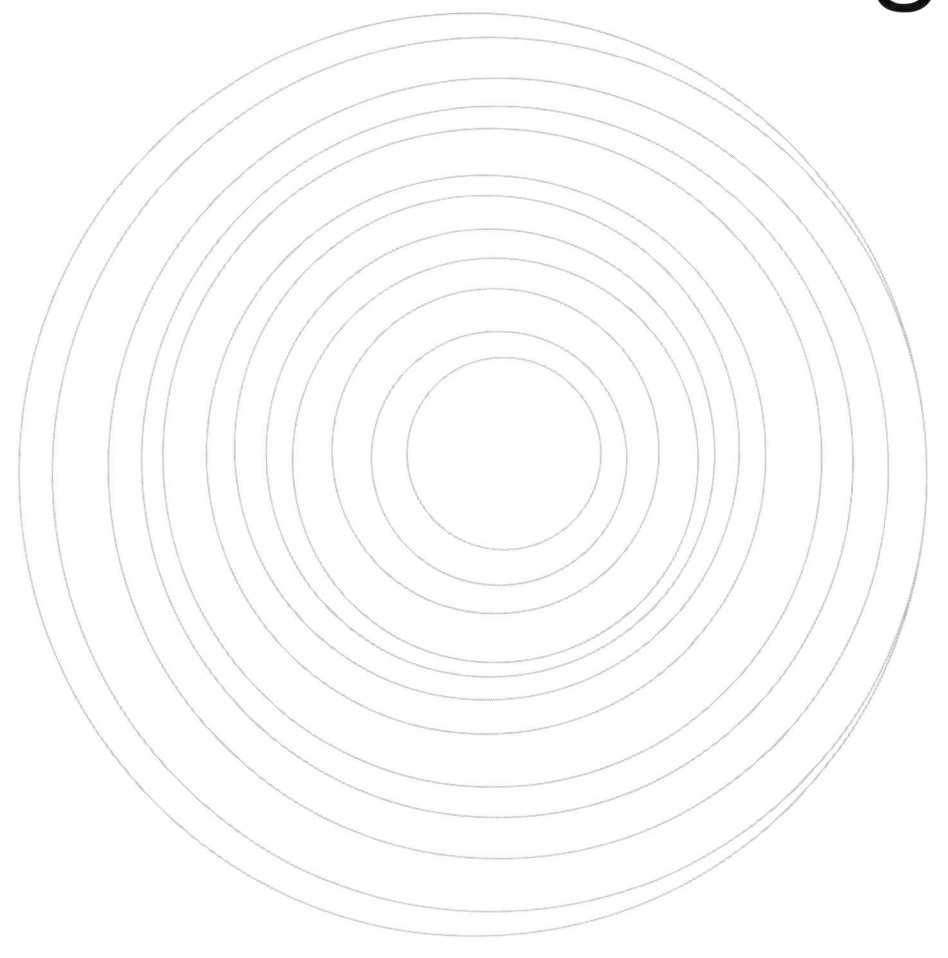

Feature Writing

Feature Writing

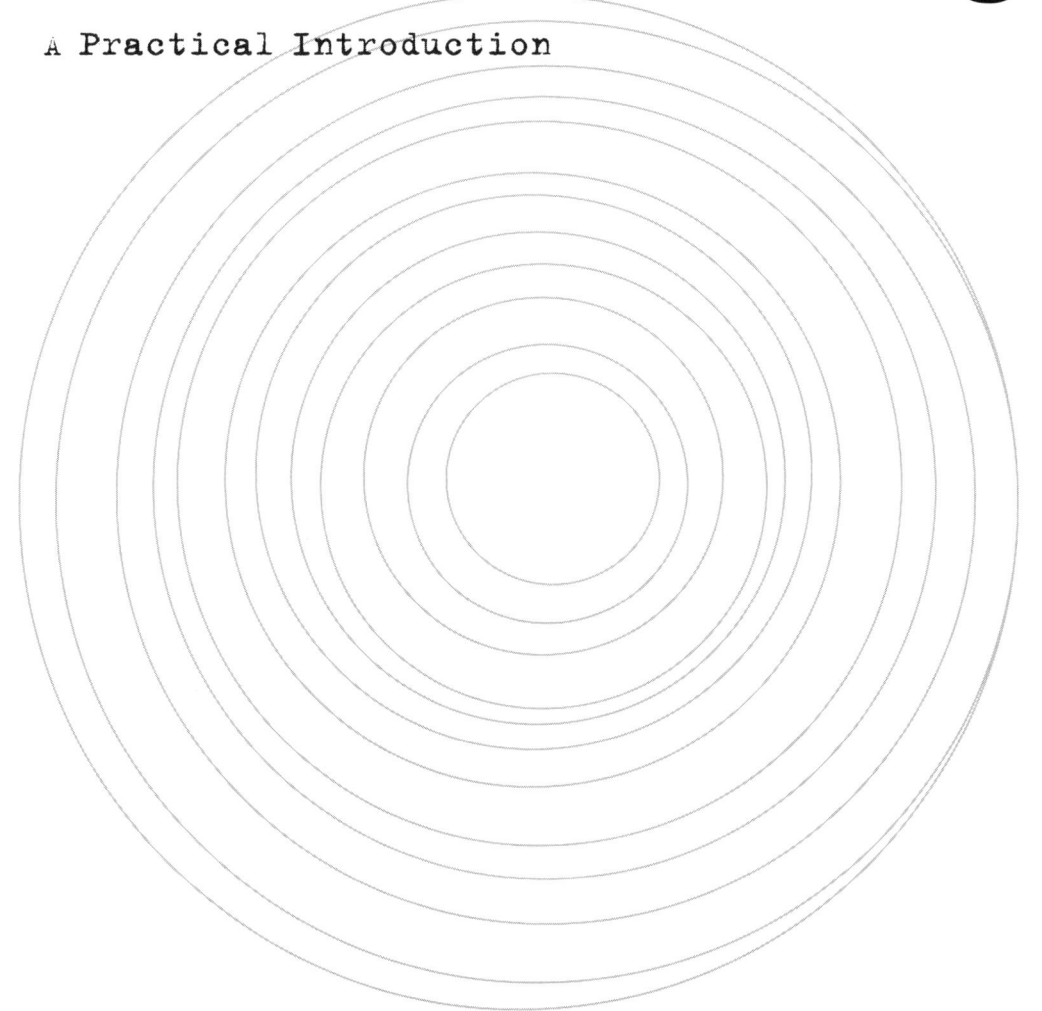

A Practical Introduction

Susan Pape and Sue Featherstone

SAGE Publications
London ● Thousand Oaks ● New Delhi

© Susan Pape and Sue Featherstone 2006

First published 2006

Apart from any fair dealing for the purposes of research or private study, or criticism or review, as permitted under the Copyright, Designs and Patents Act, 1988, this publication may be reproduced, stored or transmitted in any form, or by any means, only with the prior permission in writing of the publishers, or in the case of reprographic reproduction, in accordance with the terms of licences issued by the Copyright Licensing Agency. Enquiries concerning reproduction outside those terms should be sent to the publishers.

SAGE Publications Ltd
1 Oliver's Yard
55 City Road
London EC1Y 1SP

SAGE Publications Inc.
2455 Teller Road
Thousand Oaks, California 91320

SAGE Publications India Pvt Ltd
B-42, Panchsheel Enclave
Post Box 4109
New Delhi 110 017

British Library Cataloguing in Publication data

A catalogue record for this book is available
from the British Library

ISBN-10 1-4129-0799-3   ISBN-13 978-1-4129-0799-6
ISBN-10 1-4129-0800-0 (pbk)   ISBN-13 978-1-4129-0800-9

Library of Congress Control Number available

Typeset by C&M Digitals (P) Ltd, Chennai, India
Printed in Great Britain by TJ International, Padstow, Cornwall
Printed on paper from sustainable resources

To Geoff and Kevin

CONTENTS

Thanks and acknowledgements   viii

1   What is a feature?   1

2   Sourcing the feature   11

3   Interviewing   23

4   What features should contain   41

5   The difference between news and features   57

6   Language and structure   65

7   Different types of features   79

8   Writing personal columns   95

9   Writing reviews   107

10   Specialist features   123

11   Commissioning features   139

12   Why feature writers become feature writers   151

Bibliography   157

Index   159

THANKS AND ACKNOWLEDGEMENTS

The list of people we would like to thank includes journalists, media specialists, academics and others who all contributed in one way or another to the writing of this book.

Particular mention must go to: Sion Barry, David Bocking, Jessica Boulton, Mark Bradley, Sarah Carey, David Charters, David Clensy, Caroline Culot, Julie Gillin, Chris Greenwood, Lynne Greenwood, Ed Guiton, Debbie Hall, Mike Hutchinson, Martin Kelner, Jean Kingdon, Kate Lahive, Marina Lewycka, Sid Langley, Nick Morrison, Anne Pickles, Ian Reeves, Carole Richardson, Lisa Rookes, Martin Smith, Paul Walker, David Ward, Susie Weldon and Adam Wolstenholme. Many thanks for responding to our questions and for allowing us to tap into your experience and expertise.

Thanks also to our students at Sheffield Hallam University and at Trinity and All Saints College – your enthusiasm and interest in journalism encouraged us that we were on the right track.

We must also thank Julia Hall and her team at Sage, in particular, our copy-editor Sandra Jones for being so kind to us.

Finally, thanks to our friends and family for their patience and support.

WHAT IS A FEATURE?

The joy of a feature is that we may know all the facts of a particular story, but a slightly different slant in a person's column, for instance, may reveal a side to the story that we had never previously thought about.

D. Stephenson, *How to Succeed in Newspaper Journalism* (1998: 64)

This chapter:

- examines what a feature is and how it differs from other areas of the newspaper
- considers the role of features in newspapers
- asks how features are used, where they are used and why
- looks at who writes features.

Writing a feature for the first time can be a daunting experience. Students, more used to writing long essays, and trainee journalists, more used to writing news, might wonder where to start. They might ask: what is a feature? What makes it different from an essay or a news story? What do I need to do before I start writing? How do I write it?

As a journalism student or trainee, you might even feel that feature writing is not for you – you prefer the hard edge and excitement of news. But with time and experience, many journalists welcome the opportunity to swap the straitjacket of news story writing, with its rigid adherence to objectivity and the pyramid structure, for the creativity and variety of feature writing.

Where news journalists fulfil the role of 'breathless messenger', feature writers can be 'entertaining gossips, perceptive analysts, eccentric experts, sympathetic counsellors, bitchy snoops, inspiring guides' (Adams in Hicks 1999: 47). In short, as David Stephenson, author of the useful handbook *How to Succeed in Newspaper Journalism*, suggests (although whisper it within earshot of a news hack) writing news can sometimes be boring (Stephenson 1998: 61). Feature writing, on the other hand, is almost always fun.

SO, WHAT IS A FEATURE?

Ask a journalist what a feature is and he or she is likely to respond: 'Anything that isn't news.' True, very few newspapers would put a feature on the front page where a lead story ought to be (although it has been known), but many writers would say that a lot of their features *are* news-based in that they are linked to something topical, interesting and new. In fact, Nick Morrison, features editor of the *Northern Echo*, says features are often used to provide background to an existing news story and to go into more depth. 'As a news story tells you the "what" about an incident or situation, a feature can explain the "why",' he says. 'Aside from going into more detail about a news story – and therefore giving more substance and weight to the paper – features can also look at human interest stories in more detail too.'

So is a feature anything that isn't news? Certainly, an awful lot of material that can't shelter under the news umbrella – including TV listings, horoscopes, property sales, home improvements, motoring, recipes, makeovers and fashion – does fit best on the feature pages – albeit under the guise of lifestyle, women's and other specialist interest pages and supplements.

> David Stephenson turns to the dictionary for his definition of a feature. One entry reads: 'An item or article appearing regularly in a newspaper,' while a second offers: 'A distinctive part or aspect of a landscape, building or book.' Take out the words landscape, building or book, he says, replace it with 'issue, event or person' and, hey presto, you have a working definition of a feature as 'an item or article in a newspaper or magazine that brings to light a distinctive part or aspect of an issue, event or person' (Stephenson 1998: 64).
>
> It is a deliberately wide-ranging definition because, although features, like news, are primarily about people, they may also explore issues or events, such as the tsunami disaster that, at the end of 2004, claimed the lives of around 150,000 people in Asia and East Africa. For several weeks afterwards both the tabloid and broadsheet press carried substantial features on the nature and scale of the disaster, its impact on the environment, and the implications for the economic futures of the affected nations. Similarly, the *Guardian* regularly runs issue-driven features such as Felicity Lawrence's investigation into the underworld economy, which appeared in January 2005. Note, though, that, even where a feature explores such issues or events, the focus is firmly people-orientated: how does this issue or event affect the people caught up in it?

Features can be recognised by their length – they are longer than news stories and, typically, will be somewhere between 600 and 2,000 words – and by their greater use of fact boxes, pictures, graphics and illustrations. Perhaps, more importantly, features draw on a wider range of sources than a news story. Where a hard-pressed news hack, racing against the clock to meet today's deadline, might expect to quote one, perhaps, at most, two sources in a piece of copy, feature writers, with (generally) longer lead-in times, have the opportunity to research more deeply, talk to more people – and quote them at much greater length. Direct and indirect sources for Felicity Lawrence's investigative article in the *Guardian* on 11 January, 2005, for instance, include Polish, Afghan, Iranian and Portuguese migrant workers, personnel from three employment agencies, a chicken processing company, a trade union assistant general secretary, a trade union and government working party representative, a migrant studies research worker, the Inland Revenue, Home Office, the European Union and the Transport and General Workers' Union (Lawrence 2005).

Despite their length, features are not wordy rambles on woolly subjects. The best have interest, focus and purpose – and they are appropriate for both the audience and the publication in which they appear. Jean Kingdon, editor of the weekly *Ludlow Advertiser*, runs a 'focus' feature each week that looks in depth at something or someone of interest to her readership. 'As we are a community newspaper, we are very responsive to the interests and needs of our readers,' she says. 'We do not carry material unrelated to our immediate circulation area.'

WHAT A FEATURE WRITER NEEDS TO REMEMBER

Having thought of, or been asked to write about, a particular subject, the journalist must ask him or herself if there is enough mileage in it to sustain reader interest. It is no use writing 1,200 words of erudite prose on something that is not going to keep the reader's attention.

Accordingly, the feature writer must focus on his or her readers and come up with a good reason or angle as to why the feature will be of interest to them. He or she also needs to be clear about the purpose of their writing. A good question to ask is: what will the readers take away from the piece?

THE ROLE OF THE FEATURE

Cynics might joke that the role of the feature writer is simply to fill the pages of a newspaper. But their sheer volume and variety means they are recognised as having a far more important job – that of entertaining, educating, informing, amusing, explaining and – not to be forgotten – giving the reader something interesting, new and, perhaps, enjoyable to read.

Ian Reeves, editor of the journalists' magazine, *Press Gazette*, says: 'It's difficult to define because there are so many different types of feature. Has it told you something you didn't know you wanted to know or told you something you didn't know? Was it compelling, interesting and different?'

> All writing serves one or more functions: information, entertainment, education or persuasion. Broadly, these can be explained as follows.
>
> - **Information:** telling you something you didn't know before such as in a:
>   news story – breaking news
>   match report – and the final score was …
>   review – is it worth it?
>   personal column – I really think you should know this …
>   profile – did (s)he really say that?

(Continued)

- **Entertainment:** a good read such as in a:
  news story – oh, my goodness!!!
  match report – sounds like it was a great game …
  review – wish I'd been there …
  personal column – you don't say …
  profile – I don't believe it!!!
- **Education:** this will improve your quality of life as in a:
  news story – new evidence that smoking is really bad for you
  match report – so, that's how they won 16–0 …
  review – well, I never knew that was the meaning of 'Lucy in the Sky with Diamonds'…
  personal column – perhaps, if I do that I can …
  profile – oh, now I understand where (s)he is coming from …
- **Persuasion:** this is how you should think, feel and so on, such as in a:
  news story – that's terrible, it shouldn't happen again …
  match report – (s)he's so inspiring …
  review – OK, I'll give it a try …
  personal column – yes, I get your point …
  profile – perhaps, he's got a point about …

As a writer, it is important to be clear at the outset what you are trying to achieve. This will be determined by the following.

- **Content:** It is inappropriate to be (gratuitously) entertaining about a natural disaster that kills thousands of people and injures many more, but at some level all writing should hold the attention of the reader – and to that extent should always be entertaining.
- **Genre:** is this a news story or a feature? Prince Charles thinking we're all getting too big for our boots becomes a *Guardian* front page news story 'Know your place: Tribunal exposes Prince's Edwardian attitudes' (18 November 2004) and a G2 composite feature on royal gaffes 'Charles' world' (19 November 2004). The news story serves the information function; the G2 feature provides information, entertainment and, possibly, persuasion. (If you weren't a Republican before, you might be now.)

Most importantly of all, readers like features and often develop an affinity for individual feature writers – particularly personal columnists – and follow them loyally. Commercially, this is extremely valuable. As former *Independent* editor Andrew Marr (now a BBC broadcaster and presenter) observes in a *Guardian* extract from his book, *My Trade: A short history of British journalism*: 'Bylines are often the only signal that gold, rather than dross, lies below' (Marr 2004).

QUANTITY *AND* QUALITY

Producing a tightly written 150-word news story that is succinct and simple to read is often a lot easier than producing a 1,000-word feature on a subject that is completely new to you and for which you have had little time for research. But that is no excuse to let your writing slip. As we said before, you must sustain interest throughout the text and for this you'll need lively, well-considered writing. Sid Langley, features editor at the *Birmingham Post*, says that the way a feature is written will govern whether it interests him or not – and whether or not he will use it in the paper: 'Quality of writing is so important. If you can write entertainingly and well, it will grab me and I will read the whole feature – even if the subject matter is not something I am interested in'. Ian Reeves agrees:

> Evidence of good research is important; a feature should have interesting facts in it, but you could be the best researcher in the world yet still not write a decent feature. You have to have the writing skills as well and, sadly, not everyone has research and writing skills. Ninety per cent of it is down to the writing.

Writing is important too for Susie Weldon, women's editor of the *Western Daily Press*: 'I'm looking for writing that's interesting, quirky, lively, full of colour without being self-indulgent, and also well crafted – something that flows beautifully from one paragraph to the next.'

HOW FEATURES ARE USED, WHERE AND WHY

Features are used throughout the newspaper in many different ways and for a variety of different reasons. The various types of feature mentioned here will be discussed more fully in Chapters 7, 8, 9 and 10 but for now, a simple flick through a typical newspaper will highlight how they are used, where and why.

Early news pages will carry news backgrounders that offer background, added information and, sometimes, colour to a news story. The leader page, on which can be found the leader – or main editorial comment column – will often carry a leader page feature, which generally reflects a topical news subject. On the leader page, or on a dedicated opinion page, you will find a comment and/or analysis piece, often written in the first person by a named writer.

Moving further into the paper, you will find general and specialist features. General features are just that: features on general interest topics, while specialist features are those that cover specialities such as health, transport, education and the environment. Depending on their size, some newspapers will only carry one or two features of either general or specialist interest in each issue, others will have two or three pages dedicated to features.

Profiles of personalities, characters or other people in the news, can be found virtually anywhere in the paper as they can fall into various categories of feature whether general or specialist.

As news is further left behind, pages reveal features on the arts and culture, and will include book, film, theatre and TV reviews; TV listings; horoscopes; quizzes and crosswords.

Special interest subjects such as food and wine, rambling, antiques, property, gardening and motoring will have dedicated space – often a half page, full page or supplement. Special interest subjects are often incorporated into a newspaper's Lifestyle pages or supplements, where you will also find features including those on women's interest, family health, home, pets and fashion.

> It is worth pointing out here that there has been considerable debate around the increasing number of column centimetres devoted to these Lifestyle, or, as they are sometimes called, consumer or service features. In part, this upsurge reflects the fact that, as a society, most of us have more disposable income than at any other time in history, and, with more money to spend, these features provide a service by telling us how we can spend it more wisely, more prudently, more enjoyably.
>
> For media bosses, such features are the equivalent of economic manna from heaven, since they are almost always accompanied by related advertising – just look, for instance, at the pages of holiday, property and motor ads in the supplements padding out the weekend papers. In itself, this is not problematic since the media are merely responding to audience demands and 'no member of the audience is forced to … read … anything against his or her will' (McNair 2001: 49). In fact, from the point of view of journalists employed in producing such features, they are undeniably a good thing since they help secure the financial viability of the publications for which the journalists write.
>
> Theorists, on the other hand, are rather more concerned with what they regard as a general dumbing-down of journalism and a switch in emphasis from 'seriousness and depth for popularity' (ibid.: 45). True, it could be argued, as does Professor Bob Franklin, of the School of Journalism at Cardiff University, that 'news media have increasingly become part of the entertainment industry' (Franklin 1997: 4). However, as McNair also points out, for most people 'some anecdote, a little scandal, a little gossip is part of what makes the world go round'. Further, he says, 'the rise in consumer and lifestyle coverage might just as readily be interpreted as the *positive*
>
> *(Continued)*

> *(Continued)*
>
> influence on journalistic agendas of the rise in feminism, bringing with it a new visibility for what were once dismissed as "women's issues"' (McNair 2001: 47, 48).
>
> Indeed, while Franklin may see it as a matter of concern that journalists 'are more concerned to report stories which interest the public than stories which are in the public interest' (Franklin 1997: 4), it could equally be argued that one's view of what constitutes public interest depends on where one stands in the social and economic pecking order. Yes, a lifestyle feature on '101 ways with mince' could be dismissed as 'infotainment' (ibid.: 4) but, to the 30-something single mum, with four hungry kids and a couple of quid in her purse, such 'infotainment' provides food for thought.

Finally, personal columns are another part of the features mix. These may range from the measured, balanced comment or analysis pieces of either the leader or 'op ed' (literally, opposite the editorial) pages, to the 'this-is-my-life-warts-and-all' lifestyle columns of, for instance, David Ward of the *Pontefract and Castleford Express* and the personal rants of, say, Julie Burchill.

> The *Birmingham Post* produces between eight and ten feature pages daily. Features editor Sid Langley says features are judged to be anything that isn't news and includes news-based and general features; opinion, comment and analysis pieces; articles on the arts, culture, food and wine; reviews; TV listings; and the letters page. Midweek the paper produces a 24-page, tabloid insert devoted to lifestyle features; a 48-page property supplement is produced on Fridays; and a 12 to 16-page Weekend section contains a colour magazine-type mix of features including profiles, and articles on food, wine, rambling, chess, family health and antiques

WHO IS THE FEATURE WRITER?

Larger newspapers have a features department consisting of a features editor and one or more feature writers. Some newspapers will have specialist reporters, who also write features on their specialist subject, but often too, journalists from the general reporting pool will be asked to contribute features.

On smaller newspapers, where there is no dedicated features department, features are written by the general reporting staff. However on many larger newspapers, freelance journalists will also contribute features, as will guest writers invited to write on a particular subject either regularly or on a one-off basis.

Exercise

We said at the beginning of this chapter that a lot of features are news-based. Which of these news stories (all of which appeared in the *Guardian* on Thursday, 13 January 2005) could be developed as a feature for a regional weekly or evening paper? What would be its purpose (entertainment, education, information or persuasion) and who would you interview?

1 **Hard labour:** a survey reveals that for the majority of women giving birth in British hospitals the experience comes as an unpleasant shock – with many spending their labour strapped to a machine, feeling like part of a conveyor belt.
2 **School league tables:** the 2004 GSCE results show that, while selective schools come out top in 'raw data' exam results, comprehensives dominate the 'added value' league table and the 'most improved' schools list.
3 **Harry the Nazi:** Prince Harry was forced to apologise after he was photographed dressed as a member of Rommel's Afrika Korps at a fancy dress party, two weeks before the 60th anniversary of the liberation of Auschwitz, the Nazi concentration camp where more than a million Jews were murdered.

SOURCING THE FEATURE

A journalist's work involves a constant tension between nurture and trust and maintaining scepticism. This is nowhere clearer than in the relationship between reporters and sources.

K. Sanders, *Ethics and Journalism* (2004: 10)

This chapter:

- considers where journalists get their ideas and information

- examines what sources they find useful

- examines whether or not a feature writer needs a greater number of sources than other journalists

- looks at essential contacts.

A common question that feature writers are asked is: where do you get your ideas? The usual response is that ideas come from all around you – things you have heard, seen, read about or been told about. Luckily for journalists, members of the public generally have not had journalism training and don't have that nose for a good story, which means they leave the way open for us. But it also means they tell us things without realising the potential of the subject and that it could just make a great feature. Feature writers often find themselves interviewing someone for one story and coming back with an idea for another because the interviewee says something that sparks another idea.

All the things we see, hear and read about come from sources. That sounds obvious. But it is worth looking more closely at these sources and, by analysing them, learn to use them more constructively.

SELECTING SOURCES

Sources are everywhere. They include the local newsagent, the barmaid, the bus driver, parents waiting at the school gate, the vicar, assistants scanning goods at the supermarket checkout, patients in waiting rooms – in other words, sources are wherever you find people.

> Anne Pickles, features editor of the *Yorkshire Evening Post*, learned the huge importance of sources when she was given her first patch to cover as a trainee journalist:
>
> > I was told I could claim my bus fares on expenses and was sent out with a notebook and pen to talk to vicars, pub landlords, shopkeepers, undertakers, working men's clubs' social secretaries and local busy-bodies. I wasn't allowed back to the office until I had picked up at least three stories.
> >
> > That kind of basic training never leaves you. It's hard work but it bears fruit. Too many young journalists now expect story and feature ideas to beat a path to their doors. They fail to grasp the importance of talking to people, building relationships, nurturing trust – and keeping contact books. Too many wait for everything to drop into an e-mail inbox. They'll go out with other reporters and talk only to each other – what a waste.

Experienced journalists like Pickles understand the importance of being known in their local community or on their patch. Being seen about the place and being recognised and trusted will lead to tip-offs. Watching people and listening to what they have to say will offer up story ideas that will not have occurred to them – but will make great feature material for you.

Freelance writer Lynne Greenwood agrees:

> It may be a chance remark overheard, a comment made, a story told in conversation or an item heard or read in the media. It either strikes a chord because it is relevant to an event, which has happened very recently and would therefore be topical, or is interesting enough to either research a little more or file away for the future.

Freelance magazine writer Carole Richardson also stresses the importance of building contacts:

> A lot of people use the internet to source features but I find it really slow. I'm part of a freelance network – friends I can ring. We exchange case histories and sources, and there's usually an organisation of some kind or another that someone will suggest that can point you in the right direction. It's knowing where to go – and building contacts, people who put you in touch with other people. Often I go back to people I've interviewed for other stories. That's one of the reasons I'm always careful to treat people fairly – not that I would treat them any other way – but it does mean that I feel able to go back to them and ask for help.

HIDDEN GEMS

It is important to keep an eye on other newspapers – national as well as local. We don't mean that you should lift stories that they have covered, rather look to see if there are any stories that could be developed into a feature; check News in Brief (NIBS) to see if they contain a gem of some sort; scan the letters page, listings and ads. Susie Weldon, women's editor of the *Western Daily Press*, agrees:

> I scan the nationals and, when I have time, women's magazines both for ideas and for quirky stories that perhaps they've buried in a NIB but are worth picking up. We ran a feature on a woman who believed her dog had saved her life by diagnosing her breast cancer (he pressed on the spot with his paws, in case you're wondering). I spotted it as a tiny piece in a feature on people and their pets in the *Mirror*. Our piece then sparked a feeding frenzy as other agencies and newspapers who'd missed it first time round wanted to run the piece too.

In addition, don't ignore the jobs section. A quick flick through a single edition of the tabloid *Society Guardian* (4 May 2005) produced adverts for a new chief executive director of Sheffield Racial Equality Council; a chief fire officer for Fife Council; a new director for Responding to Conflict, a UK-based charity working internationally in areas affected by violent conflict; a chief executive for Learning through Landscapes, a national charity that works to ensure that children and young people enjoy the benefits of decent school grounds; a city archivist for Wolverhampton City Council ... and many, many more.

Any, or all, of these could be the trigger for a variety of interesting pieces.

- Profiles on the departing incumbents – depends, of course, on why they are leaving. If they have been sacked for gross misconduct, a profile might not be appropriate, although that's another story in itself.
- Profiles on the new appointee – once they have been named.
- Profiles on the organisation – what they do, where they do it and why? Clearly, you are not going to do a profile on a regional fire service, because we all know what they do and why – unless, of course, they are doing it particularly badly and the new boss is supposed to turn the organisation around, in which case, there is scope for an analytical, investigative piece on what has gone wrong and how it can be put right.

RESEARCH

The journalist will probably spend more time researching the subject for a feature than for a news story and could find that they have too much information. The skill is to select what is appropriate, interesting and relevant to the piece. Facts that are included must be accurate and sourced. Facts that do not bring anything interesting to the feature, or that cause an unnecessary diversion, should be jettisoned.

It is frustrating to interview six or seven different people for a feature and then find you only need to use quotes from two or three of them. Do not feel that the time and effort put into the many and various interviews you conduct for one feature should be reflected in the length of the piece. If the interviewees' quotes have not offered anything new, interesting or exciting, adding them will simply detract from the main story angle and could possibly confuse the reader. If you have information and quotes that do not sit easily in the feature, could they be used in a separate explanation panel – or in a box as a case study? If the answer is no, let them go.

SOURCING YOUR FEATURE

Sources can be divided into two distinct groups: off-diary and on-diary.

Off-diary sources are like those we have mentioned already. They are literally anywhere and everywhere, and produce unexpected and unanticipated ideas for features. For example, the woman on the bus overheard talking about her baby's 'miracle' cure; the man in the pub suggesting to the regulars that they run a series of charity events to raise enough money to send a local sick child to America for life-saving treatment; a billboard advertisement announcing the opening of a new upmarket department store in town; a friend celebrating with his neighbours after they took on the local planning department to reverse a decision allowing a controversial office development at the end of their residential street.

On-diary sources are more predictable and include two categories.

1. Sources that reporters contact regularly as a matter of routine, for instance, the police, the fire brigade, schools and community groups, plus authority figures such as councillors, business leaders and local church people. Although the feature writer will not be ringing these contacts with the same regularity as a news reporter might, he or she would certainly want to contact the police, for instance, if their feature was an in-depth look at the high level of accidents on a notorious local road or rising crime levels in the region.
2. Sources that are contacted to provide information about an event or happening listed in the office diary. Many feature ideas come from a diary entry, for instance, where a press release has been sent in to announce an event – such as the Queen's visit to a small city for the annual distribution of Maundy money which is so interesting that it is worth an 800-word feature rather than a 250-word news item.

OFF-DIARY SOURCES

These include:

- adverts – those that appear in your newspaper and elsewhere, for instance, billboards and posters, etc.
- cuttings – from your own newspaper and others
- reference books, encyclopaedias, yearbooks and directories
- experts – for instance, specialists in their own field
- media – including other journalists, newspapers, TV and radio, trade press, internal communications and corporate publications and specialist journals
- members of the public – including gossip and titbits you happen to overhear
- notice boards – including those in the post office or newsagents, outside the church or on corporate walls
- political parties

- news agencies
- newspaper libraries
- press officers
- press releases
- readers' letters
- victims
- whistleblowers
- witnesses.

ON-DIARY SOURCES

These include:

- emergency services – fire, police and ambulance
- churches, mosques and synagogues etc. – both places of worship and national bodies such as the General Synod
- councils – including parish, town, district and county
- courts – including magistrates', Crown, coroners' and county
- newsroom diary – which may list local galas, cheque presentations, school sports days, amateur dramatic performances, university graduations, meetings of local organisations, businesses and groups
- forward planners – for instance, future listings services
- press conferences
- public inquiries and other public meetings such as employment tribunals
- reports from public bodies or other organisations such as Ofsted
- schools – primary and secondary
- sixth form and further education colleges
- universities and higher education institutions.

SOURCES YOU WILL USE REGULARLY

We have already mentioned the emergency services and press releases. Other sources come from the media itself, so cuttings are important – both those culled from today's newspapers and those logged in the newsroom library or on its database under specific headings. In addition, you should check newspaper and magazine letters' pages, personal and small ads section, but it's worth repeating that here, buried among the opinions, comments, lonely hearts and used car sales, will be a gem of an idea for a feature.

Cultivate experts, including university lecturers who are specialists in their own field, who could give authoritative comments and quotes and/or background to a feature you are writing. Likewise, doctors, especially those in your patch who specialise in particular areas of medicine that would make an interesting feature.

It is also worth repeating that you should nurture members of the public – and these include your readers who phone or write in; people who come into the newspaper front office to talk to you; relatives, friends and colleagues who tell you things; people you overhear on a bus; and strangers with whom you strike up a conversation in the pub, on the street or anytime while out and about.

Journalists sometimes get a bad press for abusing the trust of sources. David Ward, editor of the *Pontefract and Castleford Express*, blames national reporters, who fly into an area to cover a big event and don't mind whose toes they tread on because they will not be around to pick up the pieces afterwards. 'They give the rest of us a bad name,' says Ward.

But there is no need to be a push-and-shove, foot-in-the-door journalist says Debbie Hall, assistant publications editor with *Hull Daily Mail Publications*. 'I've never needed to be brusque or rude. If you don't get results by being sympathetic and tactful, you're not going to get the story by other means.'

Sometimes too you get the best results simply from being in the right place at the right time. Hall recalls a follow-up piece she was sent to get after a driver, who killed two children and their uncle in a car crash, received an unexpectedly light prison sentence:

> I'd done the death knock when the accident happened and, although I didn't get much out of it at the time, I did discover where the family lived. When I went to see them again about what was a ridiculously light sentence considering three people had died, I expected them to say nothing more than that it was 'disgusting' or something like that. But they hadn't known the case had been up and, instead of them being really awful, because here I was on their doorstep telling them something horrible, they invited me in and wanted me to tell them what had happened. I got the most fantastic story about the two young children and their uncle that wasn't what I'd expected at all. I went expecting one reaction and the family were really good to me and pleasant, even though I was delivering the most horrendous news.

It is important, adds freelance Julie Gillin, to remember that sources are people too – with the same needs and sensitivities as the journalists interviewing them: 'You get the best out of people by not being scary and making it clear that you're not trying to trip them up or catch them out. I always say where I'm coming from and what I'm going to do with what they tell me. If you're frank and honest with people, they respect you for it.'

THE CONTACTS BOOK

It should almost go without saying that if you have moved into features from news, you will already have a healthy contacts book. However, if you are new to feature writing and have somehow bypassed the general newsroom, it is worth stressing that a contacts book is one of the most valuable tools a journalist possesses. Without it, a feature writer's job would be much more difficult and would take considerably longer.

Names, numbers and details of valuable contacts and sources who will add authenticity, an authoritative voice, fact, detail and colour to a feature, should all be listed in your contacts book. Without those names and numbers being readily available, you could waste time scratching your head thinking of people to call, and thumbing through well-used telephone directories or scrolling down through internet lists looking for sources and numbers, which are sometimes not appropriate and risk being out of date. It's far better to have logged in your contacts book the details, personal and direct numbers, and e-mail addresses of contacts that you have used in the past – because you never know when you will need them again.

Specialist writers will have their own specialist contacts so, if you are a general reporter who has been asked to write a feature on a specialist subject, don't forget your newsroom colleagues and the contacts they have who might be useful for your piece. Be warned though, some writers are extremely protective of their sources.

> Specialist sources come into their own for Chris Greenwood, assistant news editor of the *York Evening Press,* when he is working on crime stories and features. As the paper's former crime reporter, he has built up a useful list of police and crime-related contacts.
>
>> I was covering the opening of a double murder trial and obviously there was a lot of stuff we couldn't publish before, or while the trial was going on, as it would be sub judice or libel.
>>
>> I started to collect background material right from the start of the murder case – talking to the proper authorities and my own contacts within the police force, and people who had called in about the case. I chased up people mentioned in court, for instance, a tourist who was the last person to see the alleged murderer in York.
>>
>> I drew up a big file of all my contact details and made notes of all the different things I found, for instance, I knew that the alleged defendant was a drug dealer – I'd got that from one of my contacts – but couldn't say anything about it until it came out in court. But it was an important part of the background feature that I eventually wrote to go with the ending of the trial.

(Continued)

With big cases like this one, you find the nationals buying up people from the word go, which makes it difficult for us to get to them, but it's all part of the game and we generally get the interviews we want because we *are* local and have better contacts.

TYPE OF BOOK

What type of book to use? Hardback, indexed books are best in our opinion because they are durable, classification is straightforward and, once entries have been entered alphabetically, they are quick and easy to use.

Ring-binder type books can be cumbersome and awkward to write in, while electronic organisers stand the risk of running out of battery or electrical charging power just when you need them.

If you plan to use your PC to log names and numbers, that's fine, but make a hard copy too, in case your system crashes or the machine breaks down.

STORING

Your contacts book should be seen as a store for names of people and organisations (and that includes first and/or Christian names and surnames, and the names of organisations as they like to style themselves), main switchboard numbers, direct lines, mobile phone numbers, home numbers, fax numbers, out-of-hours numbers (if different from home numbers), e-mail addresses and, sometimes, home addresses).

You should also include a list of essential local numbers, such as:

- airports in your region
- big name organisations whose head offices are based in your area or take the name of your area in the title. For instance, local and regional journalists in Yorkshire would need to include organisations such as Yorkshire Water, Yorkshire Bank, Yorkshire Electricity and so on
- bus and rail companies and stations
- churches and other places of worship
- community groups including minority ethnic, gay and lesbian groups and local pressure groups
- councils, councillors and MPs
- courts, including coroners' courts

- coastguards (if near the sea)
- emergency services – police, fire and ambulance (including press office numbers)
- Environment Agency
- government departments based regionally
- hospitals and health authorities and trusts
- media organisations – including other newspapers, TV and radio stations
- prisons
- schools, sixth form colleges and further education colleges and universities
- sports grounds and leisure centres
- theatres
- tourist attractions
- trade unions and chambers of commerce and industry.

It would also be useful to log the national numbers of organisations that you will approach for background on particular features. These could include:

- Automobile Association (AA)
- Church of England
- Confederation of British Industry (CBI)
- Government departments
- House of Commons
- national media
- Royal Automobile Club (RAC)
- Services – Royal Navy, Royal Air Force and Army
- Trades Union Congress.

PEOPLE

List people under their job/interest rather than their name if they are not well known (because you might forget the name while remembering what they do or did) but cross-reference if necessary.

Under people contacts you could list:

- academics
- actors
- artists
- astrologers

- astronomers
- authors
- businesspeople
- celebrities
- councillors
- doctors
- financial experts
- media pundits
- public (or press) relations officers (PROs)
- solicitors
- teachers
- vicars and other ministers of religion and faith leaders
- victims (for instance, triumph over tragedy children).

GENERAL NUMBERS

You can never be sure when you will need general numbers, but you *will* need them at some time for:

- action, campaign and pressure groups
- Buckingham Palace
- Burke's Peerage
- charities
- cinemas and theatres
- Civic Trust
- collectors' clubs
- community groups
- conference centres
- farmers and farming organisations
- Jobcentres
- Libraries
- Museums and art galleries
- National Trust
- NCP
- Neighbourhood Watch
- NSPCC
- parks
- political parties
- post offices
- prisons

- pubs and restaurants
- retailers
- RSPCA
- TV soap press officers
- youth organisations.

Exercise

Check the listings pages of a local newspaper. Identify five potential features and make a list of the people you would need to interview for each one. Remember you will need to include an authoritative voice as well as human interest sources.

3 INTERVIEWING

The joy of interviewing interesting people is almost infinite … I can think of dozens such interviews where, even while I worried about my next question and whether the tape would run out, I was aware that I was experiencing a golden privilege.

L. Barber in S. Glover, *The Penguin Book of Journalism: Secrets of the Press* (2000: 205)

This chapter:

- examines some of the ways in which a feature interview differs from a news interview
- considers the research needed before an interview
- looks at the practicalities of setting up an interview
- includes guidance on the general rules of interviewing.

> Joke: What is the difference between a barrister and a journalist?
> Answer: Several hundred pounds an hour.
> Boom boom.

The other main difference – and the serious one we should be concentrating on here – is that a barrister never asks a question he or she doesn't know the answer to, while a journalist asks a question and can never be certain what the answer will be or, indeed, if there will be one.

The uncertainty surrounding how the interviewee will react and the surprise when they respond positively and say something new, interesting or entertaining is part of the delight of being a feature writer. But great interviews do not simply fall into a journalist's lap – they must be well prepared and worked at. The importance of the interview should never be underestimated.

NEWS V FEATURES: WHAT'S THE DIFFERENCE?

News journalists are up against tight deadlines and under pressure to get their stories written up as quickly as possible. A lot of their interviews will be done over the phone. There are a number of reasons for this: they are often working on more than one story; they need to interview more than one person and it is not feasible to visit them all; further, they do not need to spend a long time breaking the ice and getting to know their interviewee because often they simply need some straightforward facts and a couple of quotes.

Feature writers also work to deadlines and increasingly, because of the pressure on time and resources in today's busy newsrooms, those deadlines are getting tighter and tighter. Gone are the days when feature writers could spend long hours thinking about their approach, preparing meticulously and then spending hours – if not days – with their subject. Anne Pickles, features editor of the *Yorkshire Evening Post*, says:

> Driven by deadlines, always in danger of being overtaken by events and knowing that there's nothing so perishable as fresh information, speed is of the essence and feature writers find themselves researching in a frenzy to become five-minute experts on anything from Third World debt to genetic engineering, always with an eye on the copy deadline … The fact of the matter is, even if a journalist had three months to put together one piece, it would be written in the last hour – and be all the better for it. Stress is so invigorating.

In an ideal world, however, unless the feature writer is turning around a 'today' line feature for that day's or the next day's newspaper, or their publication is just about to go to print, he or she should generally have more time than a news hound. And ideally this will offer more opportunity to do interviews face-to-face. We say ideally because a face-to-face interview is one in which a writer can build up more of a rapport with the interviewee. They will be able to spend more time asking more questions; go deeper into subject areas; and pick up on the interviewee's behaviour and mannerisms, and the interview surroundings, to add colour, depth and background.

While a news journalist will often have an interview thrust upon them with little time to prepare, one would hope that a feature writer, planning to write up to 1,000 words – and sometimes more – would give him or herself enough time to think through who they need to speak to and what they will need to prepare in order to ensure that each interview provides the information they require.

GETTING READY

One of the best pieces of advice we can give is to avoid going into an interview cold. Some journalists say they never prepare for an interview; they treat the process as a conversation and, having asked the first question, pick up on the answers they are given. While this might allow for relaxed conversational flow, it does not necessarily get the journalist the information he or she needs – and it is unprofessional to return to the newsroom and find you do not have answers to important questions because you did not ask them. (However, do not let this put you off contacting your interviewee later and asking politely if they would mind answering one or two more questions.)

It could also be argued that in an unstructured interview, the journalist gets borne along and the interviewee is able to dictate the shape and tone of the event. Anne Pickles agrees that interviewing is no more than conversation – albeit with a difference:

> You converse until you have coaxed out of the interviewee a piece of themselves which reveals who they are and what they are about. Any interview that fails to achieve that might as well be dumped. Use coldly informative quotes to knock out a short news story perhaps but don't even try to pretend you've managed an insight. Everyone will read through the deception.

> It is worth bearing in mind the dictum of the *Observer*'s Lynn Barber that the role of the journalist is to act as a delegate for his or her readers and, as such, their primary purpose is to ask the questions that readers want answered:
>
> *(Continued)*

> *(Continued)*
>
> There are as many techniques of interviewing as there are interviewers, and any 'good' technique is one that results in a good piece, so it is impossible to generalise. I belong to the minimal question school – ideally I want the subject to do all the talking, with only occasional interruptions from me. But other interviewers, usually men, want the interview to be more like a conversation or even a debate, which is effective for eliciting opinions, not so good for illuminating character. (Barber in Glover 2000: 200)

RESEARCH YOUR SUBJECT

You need to research your subject before setting out on the interview. Interviewees are generally impressed and/or flattered if you know something about them or what it is they are involved in. This can win you Brownie points, especially if the interviewee is either reluctant to speak to the media or is 'doing the rounds' during the promotion of his or her latest book/film/enterprise and speaking to dozens of different journalists.

David Charters, a feature writer with the *Liverpool Daily Post*, always knows something of an interviewee before meeting him or her. 'This can be done in the usual ways – reference books and perhaps speaking to friends and colleagues of your interviewee. Information from a book or a good paper is usually better than the stuff on the internet.'

As part of your research you could:

- check if there is a press release about the subject or any agency copy available
- look at any other material that might have arrived in the newsroom, for instance, if an author is plugging a new book, has the book or dust jacket been sent in?
- check if there is anything about the subject in today's papers, for instance, your story might be a follow-up
- look up the interviewee and/or subject matter on the internet
- speak to your colleagues who might know something about the subject, for instance, if you are about to interview the new manager of Leeds United, talk to the sports editor or one of the football writers
- look through the cuttings file in the newsroom library to see if anything has been written about the person or subject before
- check if he or she is in *Who's Who*.

SETTING UP THE INTERVIEW

Set a date and time for the interview that is convenient to both you and the interviewee. In setting the date, are you giving yourself enough time to prepare? In setting it for some weeks hence, might one of you be at risk of forgetting or of the feature idea going off the boil? Does the date of the interview tie in with the peg on which you are hanging the feature?

In setting a time, have you given yourself enough time to find the location, do the interview, and travel there and back? Is it convenient for the interviewee or will it mean them dashing to join you from another appointment or rushing away after ten minutes?

Some interviewees will ask how long you want with them, in which case, work out how long you need. In the case of celebrity interviews, where an author, actor or singer is plugging their latest book, film or CD, chances are that a public relations officer (PRO) will have arranged the interview and you will be given a strict slot of about 20 minutes, sandwiched in between journalists from other publications.

Avoid spending too long on an interview and, therefore, literally running out of questions to ask and/or outstaying your welcome. Camaraderie can sometimes develop when an interview is going particularly well – especially if the subject is one in which the journalist has a particular specialism or interest. However, as Martin Smith, writer in chief at the *Sheffield Star*, points out, don't be fooled into thinking that the interviewee has suddenly become your new best friend.

> If you're doing your job properly, they'll loosen up and respond to you as a person and not just as an interviewer. But you've got to realise that they don't give a s*** about you – which is hardly surprising, people only have a limited amount of interest in other people. Once you've gone, their concern is not whether they'll see you again but with what you're going to write about them.

Very occasionally, there may be times when an interviewee falls for the looks and charms of an interviewer. However, occasions when these meetings develop into something more meaningful are rare, so maintain your professionalism and remember that you are there to get all the detail and information you need to write your feature. (Also bear in mind that the interviewee could appear friendlier than might be expected because he or she is trying to flatter you into printing a more favourable piece about them than is, perhaps, warranted.)

Barber, however, doesn't completely rule out the possibility of becoming friends with an interviewee:

> It has even happened to me a couple of times – but the friendship develops *subsequently*, not at the time when every minute really belongs to the readers.
>
> I think problems sometimes arise with inexperienced journalists, who often find it hard to be sufficiently detached in interviews. They are flattered that a famous person is apparently confiding in them (even telling them things off the record!); they respond to the famous one's kindness with genuine enthusiasm; they find themselves agreeing fervently with everything the famous one says. And then they go back to the office, out of the famous one's orbit, and listen to the tape and decide they don't like the famous one after all, and, because they are rather annoyed with themselves for being 'taken in', write a particularly bitchy piece. I always tell beginner journalists: look, all you have to do is be punctual, be polite, and ask questions. You don't have to express agreement or disagreement; you don't have to forge a friendship; you *only* have to ask questions, and that way you don't commit yourself to anything. And, by the way, *don't* let them tell you anything off the record, because it will make your life difficult when you come to write the piece. (Barber in Glover 2000: 200)

Anne Pickles says:

> Arranging interviews is a simple matter of approaching with honesty, promising faithful representation, listening with humility and delivering to the best of ability. What journalists forget is their one priceless gift. They have one purpose and that is to question and to present the reply. No decent journo should ever pretend to know more than he or she does. In this game it is commendable – not shameful – to admit, 'I really don't know anything at all about this; will you please explain it to me?' Do it and you'll have trusting, useful contacts for life.

LET'S FACE IT

Face-to-face interviews are best for establishing a rapport with the interviewee and they are also more personal, which is particularly important if you are writing a profile or if the subject matter is particularly involved or sensitive.

Meeting your interviewee and watching their body language also gives you something of an insight into their character and personality, and can give you material that adds colour to your feature. For example, consider the number of features you have read that begin with a reference to how the interviewee arrived at the meeting; how they were dressed; how they tossed their hair; how they played with their jewellery; or toyed with their coffee cup, and so on.

Face-to-face meetings also offer you location material – whether you meet in the interviewee's home, their office or a restaurant, there will be something about the surroundings that could add something to the piece.

Martin Smith prefers, where possible, to interview people at home – partly because people are more relaxed on their home turf but also because of the way it affects the dynamics of the relationship between interviewee and interviewer.

> To some extent, inviting somebody into your home means you have certain obligations towards them – it evens things up a bit. We're not just interviewee and interviewer, we're more equal. They've let you in so it's clear they are willing to talk to you. It's a tacit acknowledgement that it's OK to ask questions.

Being at home also puts the interviewee into the position of a host, which, in turn, obliges them to extend the common courtesies normally reserved for invited guests – such as offering refreshments. All of which provides an opportunity to add colour and description. 'You get a better feel for their personality. You can describe the house and furnishings, their gestures, how they sit … you become more of an observer and the final story reflects what you've seen as well as what you've been told,' says Smith.

His aim is to come away from every interview knowing something about his subject that he didn't know before and to relay that information to readers. Accordingly, in a 2005 profile of former Home Secretary David Blunkett, he described how the blind MP stuck his finger over the edge of his cafetière to check if his coffee was ready. 'I knew about him being a blind man with a dog but I wanted to know, for instance, how he made a cup of coffee. I didn't go into a lot of detail about it because I didn't want to make a big fuss about him being blind but it told readers something about him as a person as well as a politician.'

The interview took place shortly before the Sheffield MP returned to the Cabinet, just months after his sensational resignation following his failure to establish paternity of his pregnant lover's unborn child. Smith comments:

> I wasn't looking for more scandal I just wanted to know more about him. Towards the end, before he resigned, he looked very haggard, he was emotionally and physically knackered. But when I met him he looked much better, more relaxed, and that was the line I took: 'This is how he's coping and now he's ready to move on.' I didn't go in with any particular agenda, I just went with what came up.

LOCATION, LOCATION, LOCATION

Find a location for a face-to-face interview that is convenient to both of you. If your interviewee feels comfortable and relaxed, he or she is more likely to talk freely and openly. You could ask the interviewee to suggest somewhere – although watch out if they suggest a pub (which might be noisy) or a restaurant (which might not be as convenient for you as you might have to eat, talk and take notes at the same time – and pick up an expensive lunch bill that you weren't expecting). Their home or office might be best if it's a straightforward interview.

If the interviewee is planning to fly solo round the world, walk from Land's End to John O'Groats or abseil down the side of Britain's highest building, it might be more atmospheric to meet them at the airport, out in the country or amidst their climbing kit (and it would certainly make more sense if you were taking a photographer with you – more of which later).

Check that the location is convenient for you too. Is it easy to get to and can you get there on time? Will you be interrupted? Will the interviewee be distracted (a potential hazard if you meet in their office)? If you are meeting outside, check the weather.

POINTS TO REMEMBER

Having arranged a face-to-face interview, allow yourself enough time to get there *on time*. Some interviewees might not have a thing about tardiness but it is rude to turn up late, no matter how good an excuse you have about getting caught in heavy traffic or abandoned on a broken-down bus. Apart from anything else, if you turn up late, the interviewee might have given up waiting for you and gone. If running late is unavoidable, use your mobile phone to ring the interviewee, or someone who can get a message to them, to let them know how much longer you will be.

Dress appropriately for the occasion, whether it is jeans and trainers to interview a local band during their rehearsals or a suit for a profile on a prominent businessperson. How you look will influence the interviewee and, therefore, help or hinder the process by which you gain their trust.

It should go without saying that you must introduce yourself. The interviewee must know who you are, which newspaper you are working for – or if you are a freelance – and the subject area you are writing about. And, as part of the introductions, you need also to establish that the interviewee is the person you were expecting them to be.

It should also go without saying that you must be polite, diplomatic and professional throughout. Getting irritable and losing your temper with an interviewee must be avoided even if the interviewee provokes you by being rude or hostile themselves. Whatever happens, keep your cool. Says Adam Wolstenholme, deputy news editor of the *Spenborough Guardian*: 'Getting riled can make people clam up all together. Sometimes, it can help if you see it as a bit of a game, try and find the fun element of it rather than getting worked up. Don't take things personally. They're only doing their job, just as you are doing yours.'

TAKING CONTROL

It is the journalist's responsibility to take control of the interview and, in fact, many interviewees expect this and ask: 'What would you like me to do?' Increasingly, however, as members of the public become more media savvy, they try to control events themselves by putting across only those points they want to put across. If you find yourself being led into an area that is of no relevance to your feature or your questions are being avoided, take a deep breath, rephrase your questions and put them again – politely but firmly.

> Learning to control the pace and flow of an interview is a skill that takes time and practice to develop. It can sometimes prove difficult for younger writers, who may feel intimidated by, for example, an older, more experienced councillor or business executive with a clear political or corporate agenda.
> How you handle such situations depends to some extent on your own personality and the nature of the piece you are planning to write. Certainly, there is no harm in letting somebody spout the party or company message – in fact, it can even be a good idea to get it out of the way early in the interview so you can use it as a peg on which to hang the questions you really want to ask. Sometimes, says Martin Smith, you just have to go with the flow:
>
>> You have to let a conversation take its natural course even if that sometimes means people going off in the wrong direction. It's better to steer things gently because if you constantly bring things back on line, it emphasises that you're an interviewer and not a friend, which can be counter-productive.
>
> Further, exercising too much control runs the risk of turning the interview into an interrogation. This is an important and significant distinction, since the power relationship between interrogator and interrogated has a different balance to that between interviewer and interviewee. Put simply, an interviewee has the option of walking away and refusing to answer questions – then you *really* will be left with egg on your face – while the interrogated does not.
> So, while it pains us to admit it, someone who agrees to an interview is doing you a favour and deserves to be treated with courtesy and respect. That means listening to their answers, asking questions that flow naturally from those replies, and being honest about the purpose of the interview. An aggressive, dishonest approach to interviewing might get you one good story, but it won't get you the follow-ups that are the mark of a successful feature writer.

TAKING THE PICTURES

Because of the lack of time and shortage of resources – a bugbear for so many local and regional newspapers – a journalist will often have to take a photographer along on the feature interview. Some journalists like having a photographer with them – they can be good company, they can help find the way, they can help break the ice and they can sometimes chip in during the interview with relevant questions and observations. Be careful though not to let them take over and ask them to stop if they are breaking in too often and spoiling your line of questioning or taking the interviewee off the point.

If you have a photographer with you, you can also direct and encourage them to take shots that tie in with what you will be writing about later.

Problems arise if the photographer wants to take the interviewee to a location some distance away, if the interviewee has limited time, and if the photographer spends a long time taking the pictures – and it is often a lengthy process because the photographer is obviously working to get the best possible shot. It can leave the journalist kicking their heels because it is pointless asking any questions while the interviewee is busy concentrating on having their picture taken. And by the time the photographer has finished, there might be little time left for questions.

If it is possible, arrive at the job first and give yourself time – say, half an hour or an hour – to do the interview before the photographer arrives.

ON THE PHONE

There will be some interviews that a feature writer will do over the phone because the interviewee is not available for a meeting, or the journalist does not have the time or the resources to meet them face-to-face.

However, remember that phone interviews are more impersonal. You can't read someone's body language over the phone and you might also miss certain nuances of speech such as when the interviewee is being funny, ironic or evasive. There is also a danger that one of you might be misheard or misunderstood. 'Telephone interviews are good for topping up other interviews, if you need to check facts or confirm details,' says Smith, 'but it's not the same as going and seeing someone in their own environment, where they are likely to be relaxed and talk more.'

Avoid doing interviews via a conference call. This usually happens when a PRO has arranged the interview for you and asks you to dial into a certain number at a prearranged time. Conference calls are awkward as any number of people can join in. The PRO believes they are being helpful by chipping in with bits of information or by 'explaining' what the interviewee meant by what they have just said. But this sort of interference spoils the flow of the interview. Apart from anything else, having someone else listening in can make the interviewee feel nervous and guarded.

The plus points of a phone interview are that busy people might be persuaded to talk to you if it is only going to be a short phone call and, because the phone is so familiar and most of us are happy using it, the interviewee might feel more relaxed.

Preparation for a phone interview should be just as rigorous as for a face-to-face interview, that is, do your research and prepare some questions. One of the advantages is that, having compiled background notes and listed your questions, you can have them in front of you as prompts if needed while you conduct the interview.

If you are to do a telephone interview, it might be the case that the interviewee isn't available or doesn't have the time to talk there and then. Make an arrangement to ring them back at a time that is convenient to both of you. On a practical note, when you then ring back, make sure you are put through to the right person and, if necessary, tell the operator, assistant or whoever answers the phone, that the interviewee is expecting your call.

It is always important to check your spelling when writing for a newspaper and it is essential to spell names correctly, but extra care is needed when checking on the phone as an S can be mistaken for an F and a P for a B.

TOOLS OF THE TRADE

For any interview, a spiral bound notebook is easiest and most convenient, and it is worth having two ballpoint pens with you (in case one dries up).

You might want the added security of a tape recorder for a long interview, but remember that batteries can run out, the machine might break down or fail to record for some reason, excessive external noise might drown out the interview, and the tape you use might not last the length of the interview. You will then have to allow time to transcribe a lengthy interview from tape – and find somewhere in the newsroom to do it where the noise is not going to bother other journalists.

If you plan to use a tape recorder, check that the interviewee does not mind – and make sure that it doesn't make them feel too self-aware or puts them off talking naturally.

Even if you use a tape recorder, always make a back-up note – not least, says Martin Smith, because it is much easier to trawl through pages of shorthand notes than it is to go backwards and forwards through a tape recording. 'It takes a full day to transcribe an hour's worth of tape. Unless I'm interviewing somebody over lunch, which I very rarely do, where it can be difficult to talk and eat and take notes at the same time, I'd rather rely on shorthand. It's easier to read back and you can scribble notes to yourself as you go along to highlight the interesting bits.'

You will need shorthand for accurate note-taking. The NCTJ and most other training bodies insist on 100 words per minute. Pitmans and Teeline are the two most popular systems.

HOW LONG DO YOU NEED?

Before giving an interview many interviewees will want to know how long you need; how long will the interview take? The length of time needed will depend on the type and complexity of the feature being written, the nature and character of the interviewee, and the time you have got available.

National newspaper feature writers can spend days with an interviewee, for instance, meeting an actor at his or her home, taking them out for lunch, and then possibly spending time with them on location. However, a local journalist will not have the time or resources to do this. Often you will be expected to write up an 800-word profile having met the interviewee just once for about 45 minutes. This is even more reason why you need to do your research and have a clear line of questioning ready.

> For Barber, interviewing is definitely *not* an ego trip.
>
> > Writing up the interview can be, but that actual hour of sitting in a room with a famous person who is almost invariably making rude remarks about the press, claiming that 'You can't believe anything you read in the cuttings', often telling you in a vaguely threatening manner that they are friends with your editor or proprietor, saying that they can only talk about 'the work' and expecting you to collude with them in trying to sell their film or play or whatever to your readers – whom they obviously regard as suckers – often entails a lot of biting one's tongue and self-suppression. (Barber in Glover 2000: 203)

THE QUESTION IS ... ?

Having arranged the interview, make a list of questions to include not just the obvious ones, such as those dealing with the interviewee's name, age, marital status and address, but questions that are going to elicit interesting answers such as those starting with 'Tell me about ...'

It's best to write your list of questions in your notebook and tick them off either mentally or for real as you go through them. Keep the questions on a separate page so that you can keep referring back to them easily and without too much distraction. The list of questions will be useful if you suddenly dry up, can't think of anything to say or if the interviewee has gone off on a tangent and you want to pull them back on track.

But, importantly, having made a list, do not be blinkered by it. Listen carefully to the answers you are given and respond to them as appropriate – it could lead you somewhere more interesting than along the route you had originally planned. Ignoring a gem of an answer because you were concentrating on the next question could mean the difference between a dull feature and one that could be an exciting read.

As the interview is going on, the intro and angle of the feature should be bubbling in your mind. But particularly useful quotes and bits of information will be easier to find if you foreground them in some way. Score a line beside, or highlight in some other way, nuggets as you write them down. When you get back to the office you will be able to find them quickly and easily, which is important as, with deadlines looming, you might not have time to transcribe every word of your notes.

AVOIDING PITFALLS

Questions need to be clear and concise. Avoid asking multiple questions such as, 'How did you get the inspiration for your new book? Was it from your own background – and was that a happy time – or did you have to do a lot of research?' Multiple questions are confusing and although an interviewee might answer part of them, the gem might be in the final forgotten and unanswered part.

Also avoid asking questions that result in a 'yes' or 'no' answer, for instance: 'Do you enjoy your work?' Encourage your interviewee to give full, rounded statements by asking open-ended questions that start with who, what, when, why and how? For instance, 'What is it about your work that you enjoy/hate the most?' or, 'How did you go about doing the research for your book?'

Ask your interviewee to 'tell' you something, such as, 'Tell me about the time you had to ...' Also remember to ask questions chronologically. This is not to say that this is how you will write the feature, but it helps to 'warm' up the interviewee and gives you another way of ticking off questions: early life – tick; first job – tick; present day achievements – tick; what about the future ...?

If the interviewee talks *too* much, goes off the subject, avoids the questions, waffles or simply becomes boring, ask questions that pull him or her back on track. As we said before, throughout the interview you must stay cool, calm and *in control*. Don't be in too much of a rush, rather allow the interviewee to say what they want to say. But, at the same time, avoid long pauses. You might be frantically scribbling down your shorthand note or floundering to think of your next question but the interviewee will become bored, restless or embarrassed by the silences (although there are occasions when journalists leave a conversational gap deliberately so as to allow their interviewee to fall into it and say something else).

And extremely important – avoid interrupting (unless the interviewee is going off in a meaningless direction).

OFFERING ENCOURAGEMENT

Simply persuading people to agree to an interview in the first place requires both skill and diplomacy. You might try and present the reason for your visit as offering the interviewee some sort of gain, although this should not be done in a clumsy, dishonest or insincere way.

Be interested – or at least, give the impression of being interested – during an interview and use lots of signs such as nodding and smiling to encourage the interviewee to talk.

You might be faced with a reluctant, nervous or genuinely shy interviewee, in which case they need handling with care.

During the interview with a reluctant interviewee, you might find this is another occasion when a short pause between the last answer and your next question will help. Nod encouragingly and hope that the interviewee will fill the silence. You could also say something like, 'That's really interesting. Tell me more …'

BEHAVE YOURSELF

As we said earlier, stay cool, calm and in control during an interview. At all costs avoid being arrogant, angry, facetious, sarcastic, diffident, shy or vague. There will be times when you are tempted to show off – especially if the interviewee flatters you or the subject matter is a particular specialism of yours – but avoid putting yourself centre stage.

There may also be times when you feel tempted to argue with your interviewee – because of his or her views on a subject – but remember, the interview is not about you and your opinions. Where appropriate show sympathy, empathy and respect.

> The biggest hurdle for most rookie interviewers is overcoming the convention that asking questions is somehow *nosey*. Well, yes and no. Barber observes most student journalists 'find it un-cool to ask questions; they find it uncomfortable and humiliating to be taking all this interest in someone else without getting any reciprocal interest back' (Barber in Glover 2000: 203). But the purpose of an interview is to extract information and the only certain way of doing that is to ask lots of questions. It is not, as Barber pointed out earlier, an ego-trip either – or at least not for you.
>
> Nor is an interview a two-way exchange of information: it is a hard-nosed deal between two people, you and the interviewee, who each hope that it will realise something tangible – you want a good story and they want a vehicle to promote themselves, their product or their latest idea. So, forget whatever your mother might have told you: it is not *nosey* to ask too many questions, rather we prefer to think of it as gainful curiosity.

Do not think that, as you close your notebook and put it away, this is the end of the interview. Often gems are to be found when the interviewee thinks it is all over. This is when they relax and often say something more. Pick up on this if it happens. Take your notebook out again – you could even ask if the interviewee minds if you make a further note. Interviewees also sometimes save until the end of the interview those gems which they had not realised were all that interesting. But a throwaway remark can often lend a feature the drama, humour or colour it needs to lift it out of the ordinary.

A FEW REMINDERS

Always check the spellings of names and places, and check ages, marital status and titles.

A good idea is to ask the interviewee if there is anything he or she wishes to add. Leave your contact number in case they think of something and check that you have their number in case you think of something else you want to ask.

CAN I SEE THE QUESTIONS IN ADVANCE?

Many interviewees ask you to send them a copy of your questions in advance. You do not have to do this, but you could offer them an outline of the subject areas you want to cover in the interview. This might even be useful in the case of an interviewee who needs to do some pre-interview research of their own. Few of our colleagues have ever sent questions in advance apart from those about to interview royalty, senior politicians or, increasingly, celebrities.

... AND CAN I SEE IT BEFORE IT'S PRINTED?

In a similar vein, many interviewees will ask to see the written article before it goes in the paper. Do not show it to them. Many interviewees are suspicious or have a fear of seeing their quotes or facts about themselves in black and white and want to edit them. Their interference will add grammatical errors, ruin perfectly good quotes, and knock the shine of what was a sparkling gem of information. And the time it takes for them to meddle and send the copy back will make you miss your deadline. A compromise might be to explain to the interviewee that all editorial control lies with your editor but you would be prepared to give an outline of what you have written over the phone.

Of course, there are exceptions. For instance, if your interviewee is a specialist, such as a doctor or scientist, you might want to send him or her certain paragraphs of a highly medical or scientific nature to check for accuracy. The other exception, and the only time an interviewee should automatically see the copy before it is printed, is in the case of an advertorial for which they have paid. (More of which in Chapter 7.)

CAN I E-MAIL YOU?

E-mail interviews are increasingly common. They are quick and easy, and some people respond better to e-mail questions than they would to a face-to-face or telephone interview. They work best where the information you need is factual rather than contentious, and where you are expecting lots of detail but not planning to put your interviewee against the ropes. They will not work well for profiles or features where the character of a person, a lot of people and/or plenty of action is involved.

The problem with the e-mail interview is that you might have to wait longer for answers. However, the e-mail interview does give respondents time to think about their answers and it could be argued that those answers will be better for the eventual feature. Using e-mail answers will also avoid any accusations of misquoting, and it is easier to cut and paste e-mailed remarks into your copy than to transcribe your shorthand notes or tape recording.

But as with the phone interview, e-mail interviews are impersonal and you might fail to spot where the interviewee is being humorous or ironic. And be aware that you have no way of knowing if your intended interviewee composed the answers – they may have been provided by a PRO acting on his or her behalf – or by a committee.

Exercise

You are a journalist on the *Leodis Leader* and have received the following information from Leodis Police:

> Police were called to the river Don, off Bridge Road, Leodis, at 11.15am today, in response to reports that three people were in distress.
>
> Three canoeists were rescued by firefighters and police from the water behind the derelict Slater Engineering Works.
>
> The three, who are all from Leodis, have been named as Mike Rowles, aged 24, of Angerford Way; Sharon Dale, aged 23, of Rushdale Road; and Charles Windrush, aged 27, of Norton Nook.
>
> It appears Mr Rowles and Mr Windrush's canoes capsized whilst trying to negotiate a weir that Ms Dale had already crossed successfully.
>
> Ms Dale abandoned her canoe and swam back to free Mr Rowles, who was trapped in his overturned canoe.
>
> Mr Windrush managed to escape from his canoe and swam to the bank and alerted staff at the nearby Beauchief carpet factory who dialled 999.
>
> Mr Rowles and Ms Dale were treated in hospital for shock and hypothermia. Mr Windrush did not require treatment.
>
> Both Mr Rowles and Ms Dale were discharged from hospital this afternoon. Station officer Janet Simpson said: 'The man was lucky to survive. If the girl hadn't got to him he would definitely have drowned. I think she deserves a medal.'

This is clearly a dramatic rescue, you have been sent to interview Mr Mike Rowles, with a view to writing a colour feature: what questions would you ask him?

(Adapted from an exercise developed by Paul Walker, Sheffield Hallam University)

WHAT FEATURES SHOULD CONTAIN

… the depth, imagination and sensitive handling of the human interest in a feature article will go for nothing if the writer does not have the basic reporting skills to build on a framework of facts, details and names as accurately as they would be in a news story.'

B. Hennessey, *Writing Feature Articles*
(2003: 9)

This chapter:

- examines the classic ingredients that should be contained in a feature
- explains pegs, angles, facts, use of quotes, pictures, graphics and panels
- considers the general rules of topicality and geographical interest
- looks at the use of colour, style and tone.

A well-written feature is a joy to read. It might not be a subject that the reader knows much about or even cares about, but if it is well written, it will carry them along, informing, entertaining or simply amusing.

There are some journalists who are blessed with an innate sense of how to write features; others believe they can write well but produce something that is somehow lacking; and there are many, particularly when first starting out, who find the prospect daunting and are unsure where to start. Be assured, whatever your writing style, there are rules and guidelines that can be learned and followed to help you produce a feature worth reading.

> Freelance journalist David Bocking, who writes for the *Sheffield Telegraph* and the *Times Education Supplement*, started out as a photo-journalist writing picture captions before gradually moving into features. To some extent this background is reflected in his writing style, which tends towards the observational, foregrounding the people at the heart of the story and allowing them to speak for themselves. Stylistically, his approach is simple: 'When I start writing I pick out the bits that make good quotes and gradually arrange them in a way that tells a story.'

ALL THE WS

As with a news story, a feature must contain all the Ws – the who, what, why, when, where and (the token W) how. Just because you are writing a feature does not mean you can leave out what has happened to who, where and when, how and why.

PEG

Just as a news reporter needs a peg to hang their story on, the feature writer needs a peg on which to base their feature. Avoid writing an article on a particular subject simply because the subject is there. Rather, find a reason for writing it; give it a peg on which to hang it.

Student journalists in particular seem to struggle with the idea that a story *must* have a peg – and that the peg *must* be appealing and relevant to their readers. They seem to believe that if the story is interesting to them, the writer, that's OK. Let's get this clear: it does not work like that. Instead of writing just for yourself and/or your tight circle of friends and contemporaries, think of the story as a present: you do not buy presents because you like them, you buy or make something that the recipient will enjoy. Or to borrow an analogy frequently used by a colleague, and whose source is, sadly, unknown: a fisherman doesn't bait a hook with something *he* finds tasty but with something the fish will swallow. It is the same with readers: offer them what they want to read and not what you want to write. And that means getting the peg right.

A good journalist, in tune with the wants and needs of their readers, will have an almost instinctive sense of how to peg a story. For those whose instincts are still developing, however, pegs are often connected with a time, for instance, something that is happening 'today', 'this week' or 'this month', or a location, for instance, something that is happening on the newspaper's patch. You might want to write about a new non-surgical facelift procedure that you have heard about: rather than simply going along for a treatment, the peg could be the announcement 'this week' of research findings that the treatment can be unsafe in certain circumstances, or it could be that the treatment is being offered for the first time in a local beauty salon.

ANGLE

Next, every feature needs an angle, that is, the main slant or the way in which you will interpret and approach the content. To use the non-surgical facelift example, the angle would be that a local beauty salon is offering treatment deemed unsafe in certain circumstances.

The angle must be appropriate for the subject matter, and one that the reader will find interesting. The angle might be suggested by your features or commissioning editor and should be explained in the brief that he or she gives you. This in itself will help you frame questions and start to develop the direction the feature will take.

Sometimes, editors may already have a contact lined up and willing to talk. But, more often, they will determine the angle or focus of a feature (perhaps because a particular issue is in the news) and leave it to the feature writer to come up with the goods in terms of sourcing interviewees. For rookies, that can be daunting (see Chapter 2 for more on sourcing the feature).

Interviewees and interviews do not always follow the expected path and you may find on occasion that the facts you elicit do not support the theme or angle pre-ordained by your commissioning editor. It is not a good idea to try and make the facts fit. Instead get as much information as you can and go back to the newsroom and explain why the feature does not stand up. Suggest alternative angles or scenarios.

FACTS, FACTS, FACTS

The fact that a feature is a feature and not a news story does not mean it is any less factual. In fact, facts make a feature more interesting. You don't have to stick rigidly to one fact after another (as you do in a news story) because in a feature other elements such as comment, analysis and colour come into play. But as freelance journalist Lynne Greenwood says, a feature writer must never assume the readers know the background – even if the piece follows a news story. 'Inform as well as entertain,' she says. 'Features are not just "flowery writing", so include plenty of facts even though they may be sprinkled among the background or colour. Make it a lively and interesting read.'

> While news journalists tend to stack facts one on top of another, feature writers need to weave their facts into the fabric of their story, interspersed with quotes, anecdotes and asides (of which, more later). This requires a more discursive style of writing using linking words (or conjunctions, to give them their proper name) and phrases to provide a bridge between one paragraph and the next. To some extent, news journalists may also make some use of these conjunctions – words such as 'however' and 'nevertheless' – but it is impossible to write a properly flowing feature without them.
>
> An experienced writer will use them instinctively, but those new to feature writing may have to make a conscious effort to do so. If you are not sure if you've got the flow right, read your copy aloud – if it has a staccato-like feel, then you need more conjunctions. Useful words and phrases include: on the other hand, at the moment, right now, in fact, but, and, nevertheless, however, perhaps, again, although, and, but ... and many, many more. We'll look at these linking words and phrases in more detail in Chapter 6.

Wherever you use factual information, it must be just that: factual and correct. In other words, get your facts right. It means checking the spelling of people's names. For instance, if someone introduces herself as 'Jane Smith', you need to check whether this is the normal spelling 'Jane Smith' or 'Jayne Smythe' or some other variation. You must also check the spelling of place names, for instance, your interviewee might originate from a place you heard as 'Hartlee Wittnee' but a check with the source, a phone book, map or on the internet would show that it was actually 'Hartley Wintney'.

Check people's ages. You might refer obliquely to the age of your interviewee as part of the colour of the feature, for instance: 'An ageing rock star, he was faster on his feet than many others in their 70s ...' but you would still need to include his exact age somewhere in the feature.

You also need to check and double-check every other piece of information. Just because it is a feature and there are more words to write, does not mean you can be vague, that you can generalise, that you can be approximate or that you can misrepresent or libel someone.

> It is a good idea, advises Sarah Carey, a senior reporter with the *Cornish Guardian*, to ask interviewees for a contact number in case you need to check any facts. 'Most people don't mind you ringing up to query something because they'd rather you got it right', she says.
>
> A word or two of caution though. First, make sure that the telephone number you are given is one where you can reach a contact out-of-office hours as well as nine-to-five. If possible, a mobile number is best.
>
> Second, never ask for a contact number during your introductory preamble. 'Hello, I'm so-and-so from the *Galumphshire Gazette*. Can I ask you a few questions about ... and do you have a number I can ring in case I get anything wrong?' Any confidence the interviewee might have had in you as a competent, reliable journalist will be destroyed at the outset. Instead, make your request as you wrap up the interview. 'Right, I think I've got everything but is there any way I can reach you in case I find I've missed anything?' The perception this time is of a careful person concerned to do a job properly.
>
> It is best, if you can, to avoid ringing an interviewee with follow-up questions. You'd be surprised how often people have second thoughts about the things they've revealed in an interview and, while many will never get as far as picking up the phone to ask you to keep something off-the-record, calling them back to check details offers a heaven-sent opportunity, from their point of view (not yours) to request you to do so.

QUOTES

Quotes bring a feature to life. They lift a piece of writing, substantiate and bring authenticity, add to the facts and explain, and bring human interest, colour, drama and humour.

However, they should be selected wisely and used with care. Quoting too heavily can be boring and a block of several paragraphs contained within quote marks can be daunting for the reader. At the same time, too many short, pithy quotes can break up the flow of the feature.

Avoid using quotes simply to justify the length of time you spent interviewing your subject, instead pick those quotes that will add weight, explanation and/or colour and humour, and which help to move the story on.

> Freelancer David Bocking believes good quotes are like nuggets of gold – they add richness and glitter to a feature but, to paraphrase Claud Cockburn, they do not 'lie about like pieces of gold ore in the Yukon days waiting to be picked up' (Cockburn in Wheen 2002: xii).
>
> In other words, good quotes have to be coaxed out of an interviewee through deft questioning and patient listening. Bocking emphasises the importance of listening – and observing:
>
>> I sometimes think I have a bumbling sort of approach. Because I started out as a photo-journalist, I still see myself as a bit of an observer. I rarely go with a list of questions. I prefer to sit down with people and let them chat. Sometimes, they go off in different directions and, from time to time, might need to be steered back on track, but rambling can also lead you into interesting directions.

Grammar note: It is journalistic convention to introduce quotes with a colon (:) or a comma (,) and to show quotation marks as either double (") or single (') depending on newspaper house style. (For style purposes, we are following the academic convention of using single quote marks in this book, but double quote marks for quotes within quotes.)

DEALING WITH QUOTES

In a feature, there are four main ways of dealing with quotes:

- as a direct quote
- as an indirect quote
- as a partial quote
- as a statement of fact.

DIRECT QUOTE

A direct quote is one in which you use the speaker's *exact* words and attribute them to the speaker. They should be introduced with a colon and placed within quote marks. You need to introduce the speaker the first time you quote them, for instance:

> Jane Smythe, one of the first women to test the new procedure, said: 'I went in for what I thought was a simple beauty treatment – and look what happened.'

Or:

> 'I went in for what I thought was a simple beauty treatment,' said Jane Smythe, one of the first women to test the new procedure, 'and look what happened.'

INDIRECT QUOTE

An indirect quote is where the speaker's words are used and attributed to them, but are not put in quote marks. They are used to save space and time, and to summarise what a speaker might have said in a long-winded or complicated way. For instance, if Ms Smythe found the most tedious way of explaining the agony of a week spent deciding whether or not to have the beauty treatment, the feature writer could summarise it thus:

> Jane spent days agonising over whether or not to go ahead with the treatment.

PARTIAL QUOTE

Partial quotes are shorter sections of a longer quote and are used instead of the full quote to save time and space, and to help summarise. Partial quotes are useful, but avoid littering your feature with too many of them as they can look bitty and irritate the reader. However, where they are used, they should be attributed and must be accurate, and they should be placed within quote marks. For example:

> Jane thought it would be a 'simple beauty treatment'.

Grammar note: Note here that after the first set of quote marks, the first letter is lower case because the word 'simple' is part of the whole sentence and not a new sentence in its own right. Note too that the full stop comes after the final quote marks because this is where the sentence ends, rather than inside the quote marks as in a full quote, which is a sentence in its own right.

STATEMENT OF FACT

This is information given to you by a speaker, which is known to be true and uncontested, and that can be used as fact without reference to the speaker or using quote marks. For instance:

> The New Look beauty salon, on the High Street, started offering non-surgical facelifts three months ago.

TRY THIS FOR SIZE

Features, unlike news stories, are rarely objective. Where a news story seeks to present facts impartially, without offering an opinion one way or another, features offer much more opportunity for a writer to reflect their own views about a person, issue or event. Sometimes this opinion is expressed explicitly, as in this *Guardian* extract from Salam Pax, the infamous Baghdad blogger, which positively drips with sarcasm:

> A few nights ago, a small local hospital in the town of Musaiyab was hit with a rocket-propelled grenade. Luckily, no one was hurt. But what is really funny is the fact that the guy who fired the missile went to the hospital the next morning and apologised, saying it landed there by mistake: 'Nothing against you guys – it was supposed to hit something else.' Well, that's a relief. The guy shot a hospital by mistake and went to apologise. It's called manners. I bet his mum is proud.
> Now the tragic part. A couple of days later, another coalition convoy is attacked in the same area and it seems the 'resistance' is using the same sharp-shooter. He misses the convoy and the RPG lands in the local gas station. Look, give the idiot some slack, he made things go 'kaboom', didn't he? (Pax 2004)

At other times, the writer's take on his or her subject is implied rather than clearly stated. A good example can be found in this extract from an Emma Brockes profile of Kieran Culkin, brother of the more famous Macaulay, who was in London to star in a West End show:

> At 20, the younger brother of Macaulay is defiantly adolescent, his chin bleeding from a shaving accident, his fingers dripping satsuma juice on the white sofa (It's not my sofa, whaddo I care?'), all the while avoiding eye contact through strategic deployment of his fringe.
> … Culkin has floppy sable hair and is soft around the edges as if a few stages shy of assuming his final outline. He is full of self-doubt, surprisingly at odds with the reputation of the Culkin family, which, at the zenith of its fame in the 1990s, was splashed repeatedly across the front pages as a symbol of dysfunctional celebrity. (Brockes 2002)

The descriptive prose and, tellingly, the satsuma anecdote speak volumes.

What is clear from both these examples is that the writers are not simply reporters, impartially recording facts and comments. Instead, they are sizing up their subjects, considering what makes them tick; and, finally, offering an opinion or view about how the reader should see them.

> Adam Wolstenholme, deputy news editor of the *Spenborough Guardian*, relishes the opportunity to expose absurdities:
>
> > The main difference with features is that, rather than merely reporting facts, you respond to them with your thoughts and feelings, often with a particular effect in mind – to cut through the irrelevancies, expose non-sequiturs, praise or

(Continued)

condemn a policy or action, or simply to make the reader laugh at some absurdity. But you must remember that just because it's a different style of journalism, the normal rules still apply. Make sure you've got your facts right. Research is not only essential for legal reasons but can give extra clout to your arguments.

KEEP YOUR OPINIONS TO YOURSELF

It might seem a contradiction but, while it is all very well expressing opinions, there is a fine line between being a thoughtful, considered interpreter and a self-opinionated bore. Forcefully expressed, subjective opinion can be a turn-off. Instead, most feature writers allow their subjects to reveal themselves through the judicious use of quotes, anecdotes and asides. A good example comes in this extract from a David Bocking profile of a pair of collectors who run a business selling household objects from the 1960s and 1970s.

> 'It became an illness,' says Rachel. 'It really got out of hand.'
> At one point, she says, their semi contained 120 chairs and 15 dining tables. 'We ended up with just a route to the sink and to the bed.'
> 'I think it was when the floor started to give way that we decided we should do something,' adds Marvin. (Bocking 2005)

The anecdote, which Bocking allows the pair to relate in their own words, paints a vivid word picture that spells out just what happens when a couple get carried away.

Some writers use wry asides to achieve the same effect – as Salam Pax, whom we quoted earlier, did with his line: 'It's called manners. I bet his mum is proud.' In general, however, asides should be used sparingly and carefully. In fact, as a rule of thumb, any sentence that contains the words 'I', 'me', 'my' or, indeed, any personal pronoun, should be rewritten. It's the journalistic equivalent of the spoiled brat who jumps up and down, crying: 'Me! Me! Me!' They're bores and people avoid them like the plague. So, every time 'I' creeps into your copy, turn the sentence around to get rid of it. The Pax quote, for instance, would be just as effective reworded as: 'His mum must be proud.'

PICTURES AND GRAPHICS

You might not be the one taking the pictures or drawing the graphics, but it is worth giving some thought to how your feature will be illustrated. If the photographer goes with you on the job, you can let him or her know what angle you are taking and what type of picture will best illustrate the piece.

If the photographer is going to take pictures later, talk to him or her, or the picture editor, about how you intend to write the piece and make suggestions. If the feature would benefit from a map, chart, cartoon or other illustration, let your features editor know and/or discuss the options with a graphic artist (if your newspaper employs one).

PANELS, BOXES AND SIDEBARS

A panel, box or sidebar can be used on a feature page as a way of adding extra information, facts at a glance, or contact details. In fact, such devices are useful for anything that needs foregrounding, highlighting or that does not sit easily or could be lost in the main body of the text.

They also have the effect of breaking up a page of print, thereby, making it easier on the eye and more readable. They can also illustrate in graphic detail a point that might be difficult to convey effectively in words. A piece in the *Independent* (21 March 2005), about the 19-inch waist of actress and singer Kylie Minogue, for instance, was accompanied by a line drawing of a 19-inch circle. The star is often described as diminutive or tiny and that circle demonstrated the real meaning of those words.

KEEP IT TOPICAL

There may be some features that begin:

> Five years ago Jane Smythe was happy ...

but as with news, features should be topical and 'five years ago' is history. A writer might start a feature with a reference to time gone but only to make more of what has gone on between then and now, as in:

> Five years ago Jane Smythe was happy with her looks. Today she is not so sure ...

You might be investigating something that happened in the past, but find a reason for writing about it now, bringing it up to date and making it relevant for today's reader.

KEEP IT LOCAL

Remember your newspaper's geographical area and make the feature you are writing of interest to local and regional readers. The *Bournemouth Echo* will not be interested in a feature about a hill walker from Skipton who has formed a local ramblers' group, but the *Craven Herald*, which is based in Skipton, would be.

COLOUR

Adding colour to a feature does not mean sprinkling copy with adjectives and metaphors to make it sound more dramatic or exciting. It means adding detail and description that help to explain the facts, paint a picture and bring in background. More importantly, colour allows the reader to experience what *you* are experiencing, whether it is meeting a personality or individual, seeing a show or tasting a meal. Take this description from an A.A. Gill review of Jamie Oliver's restaurant, Fifteen, which begins with an account of an earlier visit to a less than salubrious Korean restaurant:

> The waitress, a lady of uncertain, age, with a face that was a sanctuary for abused make-up and a mouth big enough to swallow a fox terrier whole, smiled until her gob looked like a row of marble beach huts. (Gill 2002)

Clearly, the waitress is no oil painting. But the most damning use of colour comes with Gill's assessment of the food she dished up:

> It tasted slightly gamey: a soft dense meat – a bit musty. Actually, what it tasted like was cold dog's breath.

You don't have to have been up close and personal with man's best friend to know that something tasting of cold dog's breath is not a good taste.

> Obviously, skilled use of colourful phrases and imagery comes with experience but good writers become good writers by reading and learning from other good writers. So read a range of publications, identify the work of writers you admire and respect, and keep a little notebook by your side, and whenever you come across a phrase or description that you particularly like, jot it down. Over time you will build up a bank of colourful metaphors and similes that you can draw on whenever you get stuck for words. This is not plagiarism. The context and situation in which you employ these phrases will be different and they will take on new meanings – meanings that belong to you and not the original source.

STYLE

There are three aspects to style:

- the writer's own style
- the newspaper's style
- the style of feature.

The writer's style is something that will develop with time and experience, but the best advice for beginners is to keep it simple: be clear and concise, and use plain language. Too many would-be feature writers (including those fresh from writing university essays) confuse rhetoric, literary embroidery and fine prose for well-expressed writing – sadly, they are wrong. (See Chapter 6 for more on writing style and language.)

Newspapers have their own style and it is important that your feature matches it. For instance, it would be pointless writing a feature for a staid weekly in the style of something more suitable for a lad's mag. Newspaper style is also about presentation, that is, the way stories and features are presented on the page, the use of grammar and punctuation, and how words and phrases are used. A new writer needs to learn what approach his or her newspaper takes to the way it presents quotes, abbreviations, names, ages, titles, capital letters and even swear words. It is worth checking if there is a house style book that details the fundamentals.

There are many different styles – or types – of features, including question and answer (Q&A), profile, specialist and background. Give thought to the type of feature you are writing and judge the best style in which to present it. (See Chapter 7 for a more detailed look at different types of features.)

TONE

Most journalists, as they become more experienced at writing features, will develop a flair for writing in a particular tone or voice. It will not be the same every time, rather it will reflect the subject matter, for instance, if it is serious, sad or humorous. Some feature writers are better at the solemn or stern stuff while others have a lighter touch.

To some extent, the features you choose to write (given that you might sometimes have that choice) and the tone you adopt, are likely to reflect your own personality. Somebody who is naturally serious-minded and thoughtful will be less inclined to write an amusing, light-hearted piece than someone with a more playful personality. This is not a problem, as many newsrooms encourage a diversity of style and personality within the features department where every writer can play to their strengths. It means a features or commissioning editor, while understanding what tone they expect a feature to take, will have considered the writing style of the person they commission to write the piece.

Having said that, it should be borne in mind that in today's busy newsroom, there might not be that many feature writers to choose from. Also, as someone new to feature writing, it is a good idea to tackle a broad range of subjects whatever your particular likes or personality profile. And it does no harm for an experienced feature writer, more used to writing of weighty matters say, to have a go at something of a lighter nature. He or she could find previously untapped talent.

VOICE

Novice journalists often get confused about the difference between tone and voice. Broadly speaking, tone refers to *how* you say something while voice relates to the words you use. There is a distinct but subtle difference. For instance, a friend passing on the latest information about a colleague might employ a serious tone if the news was bad: 'Poor John, he's been rushed into hospital with a burst appendix', but the choice of words and sentence structure will reflect the informal nature of the relationship between the two of you. Your headteacher, on the other hand, conveying the same information about your colleague to the school at large, will adopt the same serious tone but his or her *voice*, in terms of language and structure, will be more formal, reflecting the more distant relationship he or she has with the student body.

Generally, there are three categories of feature writing voice:

- expert
- knowledgeable friend
- gossip.

EXPERT VOICE

The expert voice is knowledgeable and authoritative, heavy on facts and, depending on the context, opinion. The language is direct and uncluttered, with little use of colour and imagery, and tends to be employed where the subject matter is serious or considered to be of particular importance to the reader. Broadsheet newspaper editorials and opinion pieces often use the expert voice, as in this leader extract from the *Guardian*:

> Many weeks of MPs' time have been wasted debating bills which were never going to become law but which gave the government a platform to parade their hard line on crime to outflank the Tories and impress the disillusioned heartlands. If that doesn't add up to an abuse of parliament, it comes pretty close. It has been a discreditable display of low politics. It is no wonder that politicians no longer command the respect they once did. (*Guardian* 2005)

Note how both language and content leave no room for doubt about what the reader should think. While the paper is careful not to lecture or hector the reader, the voice is that of an authority figure leading or guiding a less well-informed junior partner or colleague.

As such, the expert voice is not confined to editorials or even to broadsheets. Specialist magazines or features covering much less 'weighty' matters may also adopt the voice of the expert, as in this extract from a feature in *Men's Health* (2005) magazine, which includes precise instructions on how to improve sexual performance by training the body to be more flexible and resilient. The instructions for a kneeling leg crossover begin:

> Get on all fours with your hands and knees shoulder-width apart, head facing the floor. Slowly extend your right leg straight behind you, angling it slightly to the right, with your toes still touching the floor. This is the starting position.

Once again, the language is direct and authoritative. The reader knows exactly what he needs to do.

KNOWLEDGEABLE FRIEND

This is probably the commonest of the feature voices. The writer shares information and experience and offers advice, tips and opinion in a friendly, non-threatening, albeit well-informed way. The knowledgeable friend appears across the board in every type of newspaper and magazine, from Eamonn McCabe in the *Guardian's G2* advising Prime Minister Tony Blair on how to use a mobile phone as a camera:

> ... the next thing to remember is to keep your horizons horizontal; the horizon should never rise up like that, towards one side – it looks as if you have one leg shorter than the other. (McCabe 2005)

to Lisa Rookes in the *Wakefield Express* who in her review of *Monster In Law* muses:

... shouldn't the once-fabulous Jane Fonda pick something with a touch of class/talent/credibility for her comeback? (Rookes 2005)

In each case the language tends to be colloquial, sometimes even jocular, descriptive and colourful. The writer is in the position of a friend, who knows a bit more about something than you do and wants to bring you up to speed with new developments as quickly and painlessly as possible.

THE GOSSIP

Gossips are very good at passing on titbits of information without necessarily making any assessment or analysis of the quality of the details being shared. Similarly, in feature writing the gossip voice shares the latest news about appointments, products, issues or events without providing much in the way of context or background.

Exercises

1. Study a range of newspaper and magazine features and identify where and when the different authorial voices are used.
2. Find an example of an expert and knowledgeable friend both writing on the same subject (perhaps choose a newspaper editorial and a news or background feature) and list some of the ways in which language, structure and content differ.

THE DIFFERENCE BETWEEN NEWS AND FEATURES

Not being news [features are] liberated from spare functional prose. In place of the breathless messenger they can be entertaining gossips, perceptive analysts, eccentric experts, sympathetic counsellors, bitchy snoops, inspiring guides.

S. Adams [in Hicks], *Writing for Journalists* (1999: 47)

This chapter:

- considers the rules of both news and feature writing and examines the similarities and differences

- compares the functional and to-the-point prose of news with the more open comment, analysis and occasional humour found in a feature

- looks at news stories to see how they can be developed to use as a feature.

Writing a feature is less formulaic than writing a news story, yet there are many similar conventions. The main point to remember is that although they are called features, they are a form of news story and are driven in the same way as news.

KISS AND TELL

An important part of the formula for writing news is the KISS and tell principle, which sums up exactly what a journalist should remember when writing newspaper stories: Keep It Short and Simple – and tell the story.

Features, on the other hand, are not short; they generally run from 600 words to anything up to about 2,000 – although the average length of a newspaper feature is around 800 to 1,000 words. However, the keep-it-simple principle still applies – not that the subject matter will always be simple, but that the feature will be written so that it is easily understood. Too many writers new to features believe that because they are doing more research than they might do for a news story, interviewing more people and writing more words, their time and effort should be reflected in long, complicated phrases that are a mix of erudition and waffle. Not so. News reporters are taught never to use two or more words when one will do and to avoid long words when a shorter one is available. Similar rules apply to the feature writer. It does not matter that the longer word sounds authoritative and intellectual. By all means make the feature informative and entertaining, but make sure it is easy to read.

Having said that, do not feel that your feature writing cannot display style. Anne Pickles, features editor of the *Yorkshire Evening Post*, says the main difference between news and features is in the writing:

> Often a story is best told in a particular writing style so that the tone of the piece lays the foundations for a deeper understanding of the subject and a personal connection with it. It isn't always appropriate to explore emotions, implications or add colour to a specific incident or individual in a news piece, which, by necessity, must be brief and tightly concise. However, in a feature that freedom to explore is allowed.

To some extent, it could be argued that this freedom makes feature writing a more open, honest form of journalism. Says Adam Wolstenholme, deputy news editor of the *Spenborough Guardian*:

> While news reporting might contain bias (for example: the Prime Minister's focus on issues at home will be seen as an attempt to distract from the humiliating situation abroad ...), features can be frank about the bias. Devices such as the rhetorical question can be used (for example: how deep in the barrel is Tony Blair prepared to scrape?)

RULES

When it comes to writing features, the same rules apply as for writing news stories. The intro needs to have impact; the feature has to tell an interesting, topical story; and it has to have a significant ending.

But while news tends to be formula driven, with an inherent speed and urgency to it, features are more flexible. Their greater length and often more leisurely pace and structure allow for a more detailed analysis and assessment of people, issues or events, than would be appropriate in a news story.

> Ian Reeves, editor of the magazine for journalists, *Press Gazette*, says:
>
> With the news pages you are trying to be objective all the way along the line; you have to be accurate and reflect with an objective eye what is going on and that means the journalist's approach to news has to be neutral and straight. Personality doesn't come through. But in features it is different. With a particular feature, the personality of the subject or the writer – or both – can come through.
>
> Freelance feature writer Lynne Greenwood agrees:
>
> News journalism is all about giving the facts of a major event, accurately, concisely and as quickly as possible. It involves speaking to those involved where possible, or those as close to the story as you can get, and often to witnesses to the event. Feature writing offers a broader scope to set an event in context, its background, its implications written with 'colour' rather than the mere facts.

Good feature writers, therefore, require different skills from those of the news journalist and these are not necessarily skills that come easily to all reporters. Some reporters simply balk at the idea of writing hundreds and hundreds of words on a single topic. In a sense, it can be easier for a good reporter to rattle off a 200-word news story about something that is happening right in front of them than it is to produce a 1,000-word piece, often based on only one interview.

On the other hand, Sheffield-based feature writer David Bocking feels confined by the tight word count of news: 'I enjoy doing features and having the opportunity to explore something in depth. When I do news stories I realise that it's completely different. You get the facts and you've done the job.' Former *Derbyshire Times* and *Sheffield Star* journalist Julie Gillin, who now works as a freelance, agrees: 'A lot of news stories are very formulaic. You know when you go out to a road traffic accident pretty much what you're going to find. They're all pretty much of a muchness.' For her, where a news journalist goes in, gets the facts and writes the story straight without emotion and embellishment, features offer an opportunity to tell the story behind the story:

> I can remember feeling absolutely appalled when I read a story that police were investigating the death of a boy in a bath. I just thought: 'There's a family there who've experienced a terrible tragedy and we're not hearing from them.' I'm much more interested in getting round the back of a story and talking to people.

For writers like Gillin and Bocking, gripped by the subject matter, the difficulty is not in reaching the word limit but in keeping to it.

DIFFERENCES IN PEGS

While the peg in a news story will usually be contained in the intro, a feature peg may not become apparent until the second, third or even the fourth or fifth paragraph.

At other times, the peg might not have anything approaching a news angle. Instead, the peg might be tied to something quirky or unusual about the individuals being featured. So, when Gillen covered a Freemason's Open Day, she chose not to peg her piece on the obvious news angle – that the Masons were opening themselves up to public scrutiny. Instead, she plumped for a first-person, tongue-in-cheek approach that lightly mocked the society and its slightly bizarre conventions:

> I expected them to come down on me like a ton of bricks but they loved it. They said it helped to de-mystify the organisation. The thing is not to take the obvious approach – features are about creativity. Very often young reporters do features like a long news story but there's more to it than that and often the only way to make a feature better, is to interview more people.

INTROS

The intro of a news story should be a succinct summary of the whole story, that is, it should be no more than 30 words long and able to stand on its own as a news in brief (NIB) paragraph. In features, intros take on a different style and are able to 'breathe' a little more. Sometimes, this might be a harsh blast of hot or cold air that socks the reader with a hard-hitting statement or fact; at other times it might be a gentle leisurely breath that seduces the reader by way of a description or anecdote that introduces a character or sets a scene; or, perhaps, a provocative question or an attention-grabbing or intriguing quote.

> The important thing to remember here is that even with extra breathing space, you must still come up with something that grabs the reader's attention. A woolly, vague or self-indulgent intro is a waste.
>
> Take for example this one, written as part of a feature to mark the launch of a club for large ladies, called Big Beautiful Women (the identities of the writer and the publication are deliberately anonymous):
>
> > If you didn't know what BBW stood for, then you will now.
>
> What a statement. The writer assumes that the intro is enough to make us want to read on. The writer assumes that we *will* read on and eventually know what BBW stands for. But, sadly, it's so bland that it's a turn-off. It is the type of intro that lacks imagination and could be used to introduce any feature on any subject, for instance:
>
> > If you didn't know anything about pigeon racing/underwater knitting competitions/renal problems/failing schools/steam engines/three-legged dogs, then you will now.
>
> Given the subject matter – a group of large ladies who have formed a club – any journalist with their wits about them should be able to come up with something more appropriate and interesting and which captures something of the essence of the piece.

See Chapter 6 for more on the different types of intro.

MIDDLES AND ENDINGS

A news story gets straight to the point and lists pieces of information in descending order of news value and importance, so they can be cut from the bottom up. A feature, however, tends to move facts and information around – some feature writers even delay putting in their most sensational or dramatic piece of action until the middle of the piece – and takes longer to get to the point, employing narrative flow, comment, analysis, colour or humour to get there.

The final paragraph, which in a news story can often be cut without altering balance or meaning, is often vitally important in a feature as it serves the purpose of rounding the whole piece off, either by referring back to the main point of the intro or by completing a theme that has been running through the feature.

DIFFERENCES IN QUOTES

In general, an interviewee in a feature will be quoted more extensively than in a news story, and individual quotes will be longer. In addition, particularly in a hard news feature or in an authoritative profile, more than one source will be quoted.

PAST AND PRESENT TENSE

Newspapers traditionally use the past tense when writing news as in: 'he said that it was' and so on. The present tense is creeping in, and it is certainly used increasingly for features, as in: 'she says it is'.

In deciding a tense, pick the one that is most appropriate for the subject and style of the feature you are writing. And whichever you choose, be consistent.

A CHECKLIST

WHAT A NEWS STORY SHOULD CONTAIN

- Angle
- Peg
- People
- Succinct intro
- Who? What? Where? When? Why? How?
- Short and simple words, phrases and sentences
- Active voice
- Quotes
- Facts building on facts

- Names
- Ages
- Addresses
- Topicality
- Relevant location
- Correct spelling and grammar
- Clear writing
- Attributable quotes, comments and facts
- Balance
- Current, up-to-the-minute and well-sourced information

WHAT A FEATURE SHOULD CONTAIN

- Angle
- Peg
- People
- Strong, intriguing, arresting intro
- All the Ws

- Readable, easily understandable words and phrases
- Active voice
- A well-chosen variety of quotes
- Facts within the main feature and in a facts box or side panel
- Names
- Ages
- Addresses
- Topicality
- Relevant location
- Correct spelling and grammar
- Clear writing
- Attributable quotes, comments and facts
- Balance
- Current, up-to-minute and well-sourced information, background and colour
- References to 'me' or 'I' (where appropriate to the feature)
- Personal opinion or comment (where appropriate to the feature)
- Description
- Anecdotes

WHAT A NEWS STORY SHOULD AVOID

- References to 'me' or 'I'
- Reporter's personal opinion or comment
- Passive voice
- Long words

- Assumption
- Speculation

- Lies
- Hype
- Over-embellishment
- Non-attributable quotes, comments or facts
- Obscurity

WHAT A FEATURE SHOULD AVOID

- Passive voice
- Badly chosen or inappropriate long words
- Assumption
- There may be room for speculation in certain types of feature but use with care
- Lies
- Hype
- Over-embellishment
- Non-attributable quotes, comments or facts
- Obscurity

So, you see, there are not that many differences at all and, given that principle, it is not too difficult to see how a news story could be developed into a feature and vice versa. Take for instance a story about the prime minister's pre-election visit to a marginal constituency where a group of schoolkids show him how to use a mobile phone as a camera. The *Guardian* turns it into a feature by getting the paper's chief photographer to assess the premier's photo-taking effort ('Nice try', *Guardian*, 7 April 2005). And a feature about impoverished professionals in the *Sunday Times* ('Debt juggling: the new middle-class addiction', *Sunday Times News Review*, 3 April 2005) becomes, in the *Guardian*, a news story about Britain's soaring consumer debt problem ('Designer clothes, five properties – and £20,000 debt', *Guardian*, 5 April 2005). Where the *Sunday Times* feature focuses on the personal plight of the writer Rosie Millard, the news story uses the Millard case study as its starting point, before putting it into the wider context of the UK's £1 trillion debt mountain.

Note though that while it is common for a news story to generate feature ideas, it is less usual for features to provide a launching pad for news stories. In the example mentioned here, it is the notoriety of the individual – Rosie Millard is arts editor for the *New Statesman*, as well as a *Sunday Times* columnist and a former BBC correspondent – that makes the story newsworthy.

HOW LONG SHOULD I SPEND ON A FEATURE?

Journalists new to feature writing often ask how long should they spend on a feature. There is no simple answer because there is no simple definition. It might take longer to research a feature than a news story. The interview might take longer. The writing process is often longer, but not always. Some reporters rattle off a 250-word news story in minutes but others (mainly new to reporting) struggle to get the same copy written in a couple of hours. Staff feature writers will often have to rattle off a 900-word feature in less than an hour because a deadline is looming, while another could take a week or two to complete it.

Freelance feature writer Lynne Greenwood says how long she spends on a feature varies enormously:

> A staff feature writer often has to write a topical piece straight away or maybe the following day. For a freelance, once his or her pitch has been accepted, the commissioning editor will usually give a deadline. But features can literally take a couple of days to months, from the initial idea to tracking down the best interviewees. Most often it takes a week or so – usually because the writer may need to talk to ten people and finding them all at the end of a phone or e-mail is not easy.

Exercise

Earlier in this chapter we gave an example of a poor intro to a feature about a group of large ladies who had formed a club called Big Beautiful Women (BBW). Given the following information, write two intros, one for a news story and the other for a feature, about the formation of the group:

BBW background information (real names and addresses have been changed):

The group has been formed by neighbours Sally Tucker (30) and Jessica Smith (32). Sally, a school secretary, and Jessica, a banking assistant, both size 16-plus, had become increasingly frustrated by the lack of fashionable clothes for larger ladies in the town where they live, Exville. They wanted to put pressure on the local shops to stock a wider variety of larger sizes and decided to recruit help from other large ladies in the town by placing adverts in their local paper, the *Exville Gazette*. They were inundated with replies and decided to form the BBW group, to offer support, advice and friendship to other large ladies. The group now meets once a month at the Exville Community Centre. Here, at least 45 larger ladies get together to swap ideas on fashion, diet and exercise.

LANGUAGE AND STRUCTURE

Without an audience there can be no journalism, and we are not likely to gather much of an audience if we do not seek, at least in part, to entertain as well as inform.

T. Harcup, *Journalism Principles and Practice* (2004: 86)

This chapter:

- examines the language and structure of features

- looks at the differing styles of language that are used and tests their effectiveness

- asks how a feature writer maintains interest

- considers how features are constructed and what holds them together.

It has been said that if a feature reads right, it has been written right, that is, it flows, it has a pace, rhythm and style that 'seduce[s] a reader into continuing to read whatever their interest in the content' (Hicks 1999: 42).

Ian Reeves, editor of the *Press Gazette*, says a 'great feature' is something that makes you miss your stop on the train: 'You are suddenly three-quarters of the way through and you are not aware of time passing.' Grammatical rules may have been bent and lexical games played but the important point is that a feature should be a pleasure to read – no matter what the subject – so it has to be written accurately and well.

Good writers use language carefully. There are over a million words to choose from in the English language and it is the job of the writer to find the right one and put it in the right place so as to convey exactly the right meaning and tone. Good writers do not waste their time with non-words, that is, words that convey little or no meaning, such as 'very' as in, 'it was a very long train' or 'fantastic' as in, 'it was a fantastic concert'.

They will only use neologisms, teen-speak, and fashionable phrases destined for a short shelf-life if those words and phrases reflect, or are appropriate for, the subject being written about. For instance, a new boy band might be described as 'wicked', while the term 'bling' might be used to describe ostentatious and glitzy fashion. But, otherwise, writers are advised to avoid words and phrases that will go out of use, out of fashion and out of your readers' consciousness.

> David Charters, a feature writer on the *Liverpool Daily Post*, says that features give the writer an opportunity to reach the emotions of the reader through the quality of his or her writing:
>
> > The quality of writing is crucial. It should be as good as you would expect to find in a short story or novel. There is no reason at all why journalism should be regarded as an inferior literary form. The feature writer should always be aware of this, whether the subject is funny, sad or dramatic. Most journalists learn to report to an acceptable standard, but very few can write a decent feature or column.

THINK ABOUT THE WHOLE FEATURE

Experienced feature writers will often think of how they are going to structure their feature by the time they have finished all the interviews. However, those new to feature writing might be advised to spend time working out on paper how they see the feature developing. They can do this by listing in bullet point detail what information, facts and quotes they have and then numbering them in order of interest and importance. And of course, the most interesting will more than likely be used in the intro.

START AT THE BEGINNING

As with a news story, so too with a feature – the intro is one of the most important parts of the story. It often deals with the who and what of a story, and perhaps the when and where too. But it should be interesting and arresting enough to grab the reader's attention and make them want to read on. However, whereas in a news story it is important to get to the point quickly, in features the writer is allowed to be more creative.

For instance, in a news story about the work of a team of armed police officers, Chris Greenwood, former crime reporter of the *York Evening Press* and now assistant news editor, might well have got straight to the point:

> North Yorkshire police officers are fully prepared to deal with armed attacks, a leading police chief said today.

But in a feature about the same unit, he writes:

> It's late on a Friday night and a police 999 operator receives a report that a man is drunk or high on drugs and is shouting abuse at people in the street. Perhaps this is not an unusual event, but this incident has extra urgency – a bystander says he is carrying a gun. (Greenwood 2004)

The effect is a descriptive, narrative style intro that sets a scene, but one that includes a punchline to add shock and drama.

A feature intro might also be a statement of fact, as shown here by *Eastern Daily Press* writer Caroline Culot in her profile of the *Superman* actor shortly after his death in October 2004:

> When Christopher Reeve was born on September 25, 1952, he could not know what lay before him. His life was divided into halves. (Culot 2004)

An intro can also be used to introduce a character, as David Clensy does in his profile of comedian-turned-actor-turned writer Alexei Sayle in the *Hull Daily Mail*:

> Growing up in a working-class Arnfield street, Alexei Sayle sensed he was 'different' from an early age – and not just because he was the only kid on his terrace called Alexei. (Clensy 2004)

Note how Clensy has obviously talked to Sayle and found intimate personal detail that he has used to good effect to offer the reader something intriguing about the celebrity – but with a jokey catch at the end.

Jessica Boulton, in her review of an Avril Lavigne concert for the same paper, offers imagery and comment in her descriptive intro:

> Avril looks like a tiny rejected Barbie Doll, who's slightly overdone the eyeliner. (Boulton 2004)

Feature intros may also be used to ask a question, as in this *Guardian* piece:

> What happens to the inner city when a football club that dominates its terrace streets, helps sustain its corner shops, cafes and pubs – and, crucially, gives the area a lift and an identity ups sticks and moves across or out of town to a shiny new stadium? (Carter 2001)

Or this one from Sally Weale, also in the *Guardian*:

> Looking for a job? Been at home looking after the children but hoping to return to work? I could have just the thing for you. Get yourself a copy of *She* magazine, turn to the back and tucked away – among the adverts for liposuction and breast enlargement, Kumon maths and Sanatogen vitamins for kids – is your chance to join MI5. (Weale 2001)

Be careful about questions though – you have to be absolutely certain about how your reader will respond. Jay Rayner's intro to an *Observer* restaurant review, which begins: 'Have you ever eaten a really bad Thai meal?' (Rayner 1999) works a treat if the reader responds, as no doubt, he assumes he or she will: 'That's an interesting question. No, I don't think I *have* eaten a bad Thai meal.' The reader, intrigued, reads on. On the other hand, if the response is: 'Well, no, but then I've never eaten a Thai meal because I don't like hot, spicy food', the impact of the question is lost and the reader, disengaged, doesn't get past the intro.

Some writers use a quote to open their feature, as in this example from farmer Sally Jones writing in the *Daily Mail* about a group of travellers who invaded her land:

> 'What d'yer want, then?' demanded a filthy-looking blond youth with a greasy ponytail, rising from a blazing campfire and barging into us truculently. (Jones 2004)

Quotes are tricky. Great if you can pull them off with a statement or question that is so intriguing that the reader just *has* to find out the identity of the outrageous speaker. Less effective though if the quote is so bland that the reader mentally shrugs his or her shoulders and turns the page to find something more interesting.

Other intros use humour, as in this example from a *Sunday Times Style* magazine restaurant review by A.A. Gill which begins:

> Harold Pinter says he has given up writing plays. Ah, but how will we know? (Gill 2005)

Unfortunately, a joke that works well in conversation tends to fall a bit flat in print and if A.A. Gill, an amusing and witty writer cannot quite pull it off, what chance have you?

> Broadly speaking, feature intros fall into two distinct categories. The first is the equivalent of a long shot in a film, such as a western, that typically begins with a lone figure on horseback, often silhouetted against a skyline, making his weary way towards the place that, after a series of tumultuous events, will become his home. Slowly, the camera draws closer until eventually the rider, once a dot on the landscape, occupies the entire screen. The effect in a movie is to emphasise that, initially, the individual is not significant. Instead the focus is on the environment and the notion of a physical or emotional journey. It is only once this has been established that the camera homes in on the person at the heart of the story.
>
> Bear this analogy in mind if you choose a descriptive or story-telling intro. While the reader must be offered a glimpse of the central lone figure, make sure that the word picture that you paint foregrounds the environment and the issue.
>
> The second category aims to tease the reader by intriguing them and, again, to borrow a film reference, starts with a close-up where the individual fills the whole frame. The process here is similar to the one employed by Steven Spielberg in his Oscar-winning classic *Schindler's List,* which begins with a series of close-ups of Liam Neeson's 'Schindler'. Each shot allows us only a partial shot of this man – we see only the face he presents to the world and cannot know the real person behind the façade. Similarly, statement, quotation, questioning or humorous intros allow the reader to see one aspect of the person at the story's heart. The rest, along with the issue or event that engages them, should be revealed as the feature unfolds.

BUILDING ON THE INTRO

Once an intro has established the 'who' and 'what' (and sometimes also the 'when' and 'where'), the second paragraph builds on the information, placing the intro points on a wider canvas. Look at this descriptive, narrative style intro from the *Sunday Times*:

> Inside a terrace house in the north of England last week 30 migrants, mostly Chinese, all illegal, faced an uncertain future. They had come in search of the yellow brick road and found instead a dank suburban street in Liverpool. (Walsh et al. 2004)

Note how the writers combine the mundane and familiar 'terrace house in the north of England' with the shocking '30 migrants, mostly Chinese, all illegal'.

The intro paints a picture and adds to it with the use of metaphor and imagery – 'the yellow brick road', which draws on fantasy and the Dickensian 'dank suburban street'. It is a dismal, grey world that nobody would willingly choose. But the story goes on:

> These were some of the modern serfs of Western economies: the poor migrant labourers, just like the 19 who drowned off Morecambe Bay ten days ago while working as cockle pickers.

Mention of the Morecambe Bay tragedy establishes the news angle, but also notice the importance of choosing a term from the past. The use of the word 'serfs' provides a historical reference point that underlies the powerlessness and helplessness of the individuals concerned. A moral dimension is introduced. Medieval society depended on serfs to keep the middle and upper classes in riches – the 'modern serfs' serve the same function in rich Western economies.

Next, you must tell the reader what the feature is about; what its focus is. The *Sunday Times* uses the third paragraph to elaborate:

> Most Chinese illegal immigrants are reluctant to talk, fearful of deportation. But last week the group in Liverpool finally agreed to allow a reporter and interpreter into the house.

The fourth paragraph expands and develops each of the points raised in the introductory paragraphs by telling the story through named individuals:

> A few men sat nervously in a sparsely furnished lounge. One of them, a 50-year-old, agreed to talk provided he was not named. Let us call him Jiang Zhao. Zhao has been in Britain for a year and a few weeks ago he began to pick cockles at Morecambe Bay. He looked fit and was dressed in clean but worn clothing, the sort of garb to be found in any charity shop.

The description of the sparsely furnished lounge and the worn clothing emphasises the poverty of the migrants. This is not about someone who has come to the UK and made a killing. He is barely making ends meet. Note too that the clothing is 'clean', which implies respectability. This is a decent man. It is significant too that he is a middle-aged rather than a young man – this is not some kid trying to make a fast buck, but, probably, a husband and father driven to desperate measures to provide for his family.

AND THEN ...

Subsequent paragraphs offer the reader more facts, anecdotes and quotes. Facts we already have include details of the '30 migrants' and 'a street in Liverpool'. Anecdotes and quotes come in ensuing paragraphs:

> Last week the People's Daily Newspaper in China carried the account of a Fujian man who was taken north by snakeheads by train and then escorted across the border into Russia on foot.
> He travelled to Moscow by truck and then on through eastern Europe to Holland. He too, said he entered Britain hiding in the back of a lorry.
> 'In Moscow, there were a lot of stowaways like me. The boss (snakehead) almost robbed us penniless,' he said. 'We were asked to pay for everything.'
> The man said he had learnt to hide money in half-empty toothpaste tubes.

We also hear quotes from Zhao, which are used to build up a picture of the man and tell more of his personal story:

> 'I ran a small business selling fruit in the street in Fuqing [the main city in the region],' he [Zhao] explained through an interpreter. 'My life was so hard, one day I could make a little money, the next day none.'

AND FINALLY ...

An effective ending to a feature is one that reaches a conclusion, wraps the whole piece up or refers back, in some way, to something mentioned right at the start. However, it is important not to repeat the intro at the end of a feature – or justify it as you would at the end of an academic essay. Instead, reach back to the intro as the *Sunday Times* does in its feature about cockle pickers:

> But even if he [Zhao] stays, life in the twilight world of illegal immigrants will be tough. Like others, he finds himself trapped.
> 'If I am sent home now, how am I ever going to pay off my debt?' he said. 'But with all the money I have made, I have only managed to pay my living expenses. Most of my debts I have not even started to pay off. I don't even have enough money to buy a phone card to call China and speak to my wife and family.'

The outro here, like the intro, focuses on the (ordinary) people at the heart of the story. Note the humanising touch: just as the serfs referred to at the beginning were unable to escape the rigid hierarchical structure in which they found themselves confined, Zhao and his companions are equally constrained by poverty – Zhao cannot even afford a phone card to call home and speak to his family.

LINKING

All good features have a beginning, a middle and an end. It sounds obvious, and it has been said before by journalists and academics, but a surprising number of writers produce a feature that doesn't link these three elements.

So, in effect, what they are left with are 'chunks' or blocks of text that do not follow on or flow.

There are linking words and phrases that you can use to move from one block of text to the next to help the whole feature flow. Wynford Hicks describes such words as 'bridges' (Hicks 1999: 42), linking one par with the next. Jill Dick prefers to call them 'joiners' or 'come-ons'. Frankly, it does not matter what you call them as long as you use them to help the reader 'bridge the mental jump of eye and brain from one paragraph to the next' (Dick 2003: 70).

In other words (a good example of a transition phrase), you need to offer the reader a helping hand and give them a push on to the next paragraph. If you don't, there is a strong chance their attention will be caught by another item on the page or even over the page or, worse yet, another publication.

Generally, transition words or phrases can be found at the beginning or end of a sentence or paragraph. Examples, as we suggest below, include words such as perhaps, again, nevertheless, however, but, first, finally, primarily, and, because, although, though, at least, on the other hand, in other words, in general, on occasion … the list goes on. Occasionally, however, they will come in the middle where they are used to link two separate clauses.

> He tries to keep healthy **although** the necessity of long tours with the band makes this difficult.

New writers often get these wrong – sometimes simply because they fail to think carefully about the word they plan to use or are too lazy to check the meaning of it in the dictionary.

The following Q&A profile originally appeared in the *Weekend* magazine of the *Guardian* (Greenstreet 2003). This example shows how, with judicious use of linking words and phrases, the original can be turned into a smooth-flowing piece of copy:

Q&A

Adam Duritz, 38, grew up in Berkeley, California. He worked on building sites and shops, and suffered a year-long, LSD-induced nervous breakdown, before forming Counting Crows. The band got a record deal with Geffen in 1992 and their first single, Mr Jones, was a huge hit. Their debut album, *August And Everything After*, was the fastest-selling album in the US since Nirvana's *Nevermind*. Their new single, a cover of 'Big Yellow Taxi' by Joni Mitchell, is out now. Duritz recently moved to New York.

(Continued)

What is your idea of perfect happiness?
To have a family, and still be able to carry on a vital artistic life.
What is your greatest fear?
Being unable to take care of myself.
What is the trait you most deplore in yourself?
Too many.
What is the trait you most deplore in others?
Ignorance and bigotry.
What is your greatest extravagance?
I have nine copies of Joni Mitchell – *Blue*
What makes you depressed?
Sleeplessness. Hotels. Sleeplessness in hotels especially.
What do you most dislike about your appearance?
Weight goes up, weight goes down, goes up, goes down …
Should the royal family be scrapped?
It's none of my business what you do with your heritage.
What or who is the greatest love of your life?
I haven't met her yet. At least, no one I've met yet has agreed to be her.
Which living person do you most despise?
I'm not crazy about our president, or anyone, for that matter, who uses tragedy as political coin.
Have you ever said 'I love you' and not meant it?
Yes, unfortunately.
Which words or phrases do you most overuse?
That last one's a problem.
How often do you have sex?
Not often enough.
What single thing would improve the quality of your life?
More of the above.
How would you like to die?
Think I'd rather stay. Maybe I'll live for ever.
Do you believe in life after death?
I have no idea.
How would you like to be remembered?
As I said, I'm not necessarily leaving, so tell me now.
What is the most important lesson life has taught you?
It's a shitty world, but it doesn't have to be that way where you are.
(Copyright Guardian Newspapers Limited)

Now, with linking words and phrases (emphasised in bold), the former Q&A feature could read:

Rock star Adam Duritz is at the peak of his powers. **His** debut album *August and Everything After* with the band Counting Crows was the fastest-selling

(Continued)

(Continued)

album in the US since Nirvana's *Nevermind* and their new single, a cover of 'Big Yellow Taxi' by Joni Mitchell, is set to eclipse it, **yet** the singer remains preoccupied with death and dying.

Perhaps the obsession is fuelled by the after-effects of a year-long LSD-induced nervous breakdown **but** 38-year-old Duritz has contemplated his own mortality and decided: 'Think I'd rather stay. Maybe I'll live for ever.'

Again, perhaps it is the nervous breakdown, or the product of his recent move to New York, **but** Duritz, born and raised in laid-back Berkeley in California, lives resolutely in the present.

'I have no idea if there is life after death,' he said. **Nor** is he interested in how others will talk about him after he is gone. 'I'm not necessarily leaving, so tell me now how I'll be remembered.'

His preoccupations reflect his fears about life, his ability to continue to produce good music and the essential loneliness at the core of his being. His idea of perfect happiness, **though**, would be to have a family: 'And still be able to carry on a vital artistic life.'

But such ambitions remain in the future. He freely admits that he has not yet met the greatest love of his life. **Or, at least**, he acknowledges: 'No one I've met yet has agreed to be her.'

Partly, he blames the absence of a significant other on his own failure to fully commit to a relationship. There have been times, he says, when he has said 'I love you' and not meant it.

Again, this lack of commitment could have its roots in his earlier breakdown that preceded the formation of Counting Crows, their 1992 record deal with Geffen and their first massive hit single, 'Mr Jones'.

His greatest fear is that he may, one day, be unable to look after himself. He tries to keep healthy **although** the necessity of long tours with the band makes this difficult. 'Weight goes up, weight goes down, goes up, goes down …' his voice trails off. He is plagued by sleeplessness **too**. 'In hotels, especially.'

Nevertheless, he remains essentially optimistic: 'The most important lesson life has taught me is it's a shitty world, but it doesn't have to be that way where you are.'

AND WHAT HAPPENED TO SO-AND-SO?

If you fail to make links in your feature writing, you will leave the reader with unanswered questions. For instance, some writers make the mistake of introducing an element at the start of their feature and then never referring back to it, leaving the reader to question what happened to so-and-so.

It will help to create cohesion and copy flow if you run a theme through the whole feature and you can do this by introducing a theme in your intro and following it through or referring to it elsewhere at intervals in the text – and then by coming back to it for the wrap-up at the end. Using a theme, which by the end of the feature will be familiar to the reader, will help to 'close off' the article in the reader's mind.

Hull Daily Mail reporter Jessica Boulton used the theme of travel to tell the story of a female lorry driver who had been named the nation's best woman trucker. While it is fairly obvious that 'travel' would be the theme of such an article, it is worth looking at the specific words and phrases that Boulton has used (the thematic words and phrases are highlighted in bold). Notice how they fit the piece, offer a play on words, keep reminding us of the theme and move the whole feature on. Boulton begins:

> It's 8am on a Monday and **trucker** Kimberley Duncalf has been **on the road** for three hours.
> This is the start of her working week and she won't **return** to her Market Weighton **home** for another five days.
> Ahead of her lies **hundreds of miles of motorway**, four nights of sleeping in her **cab** and numerous cups of tea in **truckers' cafes**.
> It will be Saturday morning when she next sees boyfriend Shaun, 35.
> But for Kimberley there's no job on this Earth she would rather have than that of a **lorry driver**.
> The 32-year-old scooped the top honour at the **Women in Transport Road Haulage Association** awards last week, but today is back **revving** with excitement as she talks on the **car-phone** about the perks of the job.
> '**On the road**, you're your own boss, you can **watch the world go by**, you **travel all over the country** and **see places** you would never otherwise see,' said Kimberley.

Boulton continues in this vein throughout the article and finally ties up the loose ends thus:

> Kimberley has now made the job her own. Last week her hard work earned her the national prize for Operational Excellence at the **Women in Transport** awards. She was presented with a silver salver, crystal fruit bowl and £250 in vouchers at London's Savoy Hotel.
> Today, as Kimberley **heads down south**, the salver is at **home**, in Market Weighton, being polished daily by proud boyfriend Shaun.
> The pair met when he worked at a **truckers' agency** and gave freelance jobs to Kimberley.
> 'I miss him when I'm **on the road** but it makes us value the time we have together more,' she said.
> With such enthusiasm for her job, precious little is going to make Kimberley give it up – except children.
> 'If we start a family I'll have to give it up,' she says regretfully. 'I cannot imagine me being allowed to put a baby seat in the **cab**. But that will not be for a while.'
> Putting the **future** to the back of her mind, the **trucker** hangs up the **car-phone** and **happily ploughs down the motorway**.

DID HE SAY IT OR WAS IT SAID?

As we said in Chapter 5 when we looked at some of the main differences between writing news stories and features, the past tense is commonly used in news while the present tense is more often used in features.

A feature writer needs to decide whether to write in the past or present tense and often the theme and style of the feature will help make the decision. There are some features that lend themselves to the more formal past tense presentation, while others read more comfortably in the present. However, whether past or present is chosen, the tense must be used consistently.

> Note that certain conventions apply to writing reviews. It is customary to use the present tense when reviewing an ongoing work, such as a book or a long-running play or the first night of a 30-gig band tour; and the past tense for one-off performances or screenings or productions that have completed their run. Television reviewers, for instance, always write in the past tense. Film reviewers tend to use the present. (See Chapter 9 for more on writing reviews.)

SHE SAID, CLAIMED, ADDED, SOBBED AND SIGHED

Trainee reporters are often concerned about using the word 'said' to introduce every quote in a news story – they think it will jar with repetition. They therefore try to find alternatives to stop the reader becoming bored. But actually, 'said' is the best word to use when introducing one or two quotes in a short news piece.

However, in features, we expect to include more quotes – and quotes from more sources – and the overuse of the word 'said' could become irritating. Think of substitutes by all means, but make sure they are appropriate to the sense of what you are writing and that they fit the tone and style of the piece. With that in mind, substitutes such as 'commented', 'claimed', 'added', 'went on' and 'remarked' will work. Beware, though, that alternatives such as 'agreed', 'added' and 'claimed' have specific meanings and should only be used to make those meanings clear.

Use 'she sobbed', 'he laughed' and the like if it fits the tone of the article but try not to overdo it.

WORD LENGTH

Newspaper features can have a word length of anything from about 600 to about 2,000 words (although few local or regional newspapers have the space to carry features of more than about 1,200 words). The average word length is more likely to be between 800 and 1,500 words. Always ask how many words are needed and then stick to the length given.

Don't think that the feature should reflect in length the time you have spent researching, interviewing and writing it, because it will only end up being cut to the length that was required. If you feel strongly that you have plenty to say and can better say it in a longer word length, try to convince your commissioning editor to give you more space.

However, it is worth learning how to differentiate between the important bits of research that you can successfully use and those that don't add anything to the overall piece. Do not be too proud or precious to jettison some of your research, however hard-earned.

GET WRITING

Those new to feature writing – and some not so new – can find any number of reasons and excuses not to start writing their feature straight away. It can be a daunting prospect to be faced with pages of interview notes and research, and not know where to start. It is remarkable, too, just how many things a journalist can find to do that are more important than starting to write: have a coffee or lunch, study the small ads in that day's paper, hang the washing out and clean the loo (these last two used more often as delaying tactics by feature writers who are female and freelance). But you will more than likely be up against a deadline and your feature could be needed for the next edition of the paper, so you don't have the luxury of delaying.

Whatever the case, our advice is to write up your copy as soon as possible after doing your interviews, while the information is fresh and the 'atmosphere' of the interview can still be felt. Because of the nature of researching a feature, you will probably have more information than you need and the longer you delay, the more confusing that information will look.

However, if an intro, angle or theme has not occurred to you by now, read through your notes, highlighting quotes that leapt out at you at the time of the interview – or leap out at you now – and listing facts in order of importance and interest.

To help, imagine you are telling a friend about the interview and what you have found out about the subject. Think what you would tell them first to get them to stop and listen to you; hit them with the facts that you found the most interesting; recount the anecdotes that interested you the most; and include the quotes you felt added best to the story.

Exercise

We mentioned the importance of linking words and phrases earlier. Pick out a feature you have enjoyed reading recently and go through it underlining the linking words and phrases. You'll see how they help to provide a bridge between the disparate ideas and details in one paragraph and the next.

Now, find an example of a Q&A profile. Can you use linking words and phrases to link these quotes together? You don't necessarily have to use the quotes in the order in which they appear, but judicious use of conjunctions will enable you to create a flowing piece of copy.

DIFFERENT TYPES OF FEATURES

Readers approach features very much as they approach food. Some want simple grub, some fancy cooking, some heavy stodge. Very few relish stale cheese sandwiches or froth. To labour the simile, good ingredients and preparation are essential.

D. Stephenson, *How to Succeed in Newspaper Journalism* (1998: 50)

This chapter:

- examines some of the different categories of features
- looks at news features and backgrounders
- considers the use of profiles and personal columns
- looks at reviews and advertorials
- studies general differences in style.

The different categories of features are many and various, and range from serious pieces of political analysis to articles about local pop groups, and from stories about toddlers triumphing over tragedy to profiles of local entrepreneurs succeeding in business. Subjects range from the serious to the silly, from the bleakest of life to the light-hearted, and from topics of national importance to snippets about kitchenware. Features include subjects as diverse as TV, book, play, cinema and restaurant reviews; business; politics; travel; gardening; motoring; arts; culture; horoscopes; diet; and fashion.

And while we would hesitate to say that features are everything in a newspaper that isn't news, we would have to agree that much of the material that isn't strictly categorised as news does end up on the feature pages.

NEWS BACKGROUNDER

A news backgrounder is an important feature in that it is what it says it is: a background to the news. News backgrounders offer extra information and detail on the people or the events that are carried in a news story elsewhere in the newspaper. For instance, a hard news story of about 250 to 400 words carried on the front page might include a note at the end referring the reader to a backgrounder carried inside the newspaper, or, if the news story is on an inside news page, the backgrounder will often be positioned alongside or below it on the same page.

Backgrounders are usually about 600 words in length and offer added information, insight, explanation, colour and/or analysis. They often consider the repercussions of a situation or an event featured in the main news story, that is, how the situation or event has affected or will affect people – what are the causes and effect – and what might happen next.

The backgrounder might also consider other linked or similar events, for instance, a backgrounder to accompany a main news story about a rail crash that has occurred in the region might also give details of rail crashes that have occurred within the last few months elsewhere in the country.

COLOUR

A news story might have a news backgrounder to accompany it or, depending on the subject matter, it might have a colour piece alongside it. A colour piece typically looks behind the scenes of an event to focus on something unusual, entertaining or quirky. For instance, in the event of a royal visit to your town, you might be asked to write a colour piece, which could include details of the number and type of vehicles used in the regal motorcade, what a particular royal was wearing, or what particular flowers went into the many bouquets that were presented to him or her. You might also report conversations that took place between their majesties and local people to whom they were introduced (bearing in mind that you would have to get these details later as you probably would not be able to get close enough to eavesdrop at the time).

You might suppose that a colour piece involves colourful writing, but this is not the case and it certainly does not mean you can go overboard with metaphors, clichés and over-use of adjectives.

> Although colour pieces will typically appear on the same day as the accompanying news story, they sometimes function as previews, contributing to the dramatic build-up before a big event. Three weeks before the Queen's 2005 Maundy Thursday visit to Wakefield Cathedral, for instance, the *Wakefield Express* ran a short colour piece ('Queen's visit – latest', 4 March 2005) detailing police plans to close several of the city's car parks as part of their security plans. Two weeks later they ran another piece about the order of service and the next week, when she actually came, they had a 16-page supplement that included articles on the history of the Maundy Thursday service, a description of the service itself, mini profiles of some of the people involved and a backgrounder on where the Maundy money is made, and, a couple of weeks after that, they ran follow-up stories about Maundy money going on sale on eBay.

FOLLOW-UP FEATURE

The follow-up feature follows a main news story, but unlike a backgrounder, not on the same day of publication. A follow-up feature would pick up on a particular angle or point in the main news story and develop it for use some time over the next few days. For instance, a newspaper that carries a main news story about a family from the region who had a 'miraculous escape' in a coach crash while on holiday abroad, would not only do a follow-up story when the family returned home, but might include a follow-up feature with quotes and pictures that tells more about the family – who they are, what they had been doing on holiday, how the crash happened and how they had 'miraculously' survived.

A follow-up feature may also be used weeks, months and, sometimes, years after the main news story connected to it has appeared in the newspaper, for instance, to mark anniversaries. A follow-up feature would be used to remind readers that it is exactly a year since a particular train crash in the region in which a number of people died. It would include interviews with survivors and victims' relatives to see how they had recovered and coped in the previous 12 months, and with representatives from the rail industry to see what changes had been made to make rail travel safer and so on.

A follow-up feature would also be used on the birthday, or on the anniversary of the date on which a child went missing, for instance, to hear how the parents and the rest of the family were coping, to remind readers that the child had not yet been found, and to help re-ignite or keep the hunt for him or her alive.

LEADER PAGE

The leader page of a newspaper is important in that it carries the leaders or editorials – usually a column made up of one, two or three separate comment pieces on the important news issues of the day. Generally, they will be written by the editor or perhaps, a specialist leader writer or senior reporter. In all cases, the leader reflects the opinion of the paper, as determined by the editor (or proprietor) and not the voice of an individual journalist. As such, they do not carry a byline and instead appear under a copy of the paper's masthead.

> David Stephenson describes editorials as the 'something to be done column' (Stephenson 1998: 99). It is a good description since it emphasises the role of a leader as a vehicle to influence and lead public opinion. Essentially, the leader identifies an issue of interest to its community of readers and offers an opinion on how it should be resolved. While the tone of broadsheet leaders tends to be measured, balanced and objective, albeit opinionated, tabloid editorials are subjective and, sometimes, brutally direct. Crucially, both types of editorial leave the reader in absolutely no doubt about what they should think about an issue or what someone, usually the government, should do about it.

A feature on the leader page, which sits alongside the editorial column, is one that analyses and delves deeper into the important news issues of the day. But it goes further than a news backgrounder, in that it can also contain the writer's own comments. Often leader page features will be written by newspaper staff, but, depending on the subject, a guest writer such as someone with specific, expert knowledge on the subject being aired will be invited to write it.

PROFILING THE CELEBRITY

Profiles involve personalities, celebrities and characters, who have done something new, unusual or extraordinary. Writing a profile gives a feature writer the chance to meet all types of people not usually available to the general public. The list includes major (and minor) stars and wannabes from the world of film, theatre and music, authors, artists, politicians, and experts from specialist fields such as science, medicine and astronomy.

The important point to remember when writing a profile is that you are only getting a snapshot of your interviewee – you don't have time to get to know them properly – and they are only doing the interview because they want (or have been told by their publicist) to promote their latest film, play, CD, book or breakthrough. Often, a personality will be doing the rounds as part of a film, play or book tour, visiting different towns and cities to put themselves at the mercy of the interviewing techniques of the many and various local and regional feature writers who want to spotlight them in their newspaper.

Your newspaper may have been told about an interview opportunity by way of a press release, which will contain a time and date (because the celebrity will only be in your region for a short time) and a location (usually either the foyer of, or a room in, a local hotel). In the case of a big-name interview, you might be restricted to just 20 minutes with the interviewee, in which case, plan your questions carefully. Remember also that you will be in a line of journalists conducting interviews that day, so you may be kept waiting for your turn if those before you overrun, or you may be hurried out if there are several journalists coming up behind you.

Often in the case of a mega-celebrity, a public relations officer (PRO) or publicist will want to sit in on the interview. Avoid this if you can, as a pushy third presence in the room can put the celebrity off or put you off, or just as bad, take over and suggest answers to your questions or prevent you from asking certain questions.

Interviews with celebrities run the risk of producing what Fleet Street doyenne Lynn Barber describes as the 'Tell me, Famous Person, what brings you to London' style of profile (Barber in Glover 2000: 196). Pushed for time, it can be hard for even the most experienced journalist to elicit new or revealing responses. Editors, however, still want entertaining copy and so the flip-side for writers is, as Barber observes, that, to 'fill the gap between the three interesting sentences the star has uttered and the 3,000-word whole needed to provide a selling magazine cover story, writers are encouraged to indulge in whatever diversions they can invent along the way' (ibid.: 199).

Accordingly, the *Guardian*'s Simon Hattenstone, who, because of traffic hold-ups, missed his allotted slot with Dame Judi Dench, weaves details of his frustrating attempts to conduct the interview via mobile phone into an unconventional, but, ultimately, satisfying profile of the actress:

Dame Judi, in brief

She's the grande dame of British theatre, doesn't suffer fools and rarely gives interviews. So when Simon Hattenstone got one, he was determined to be on time for Judi Dench. Only he didn't take into account the traffic on the A40. So just how many questions can you fit into 30 seconds?

So many questions, so little time. We're on the road to Cheltenham to meet Judi Dench. Dame Judi, the legend of stage and screen. We've been given half an hour with her – just before Dench, the new president of the Cheltenham Book Festival, will address an audience of 1,700 on Shakespeare.

Is she really as queenly and cold as she seems at times (not least when playing Queens Victoria and Elizabeth)? Is she as impetuous and hot-blooded as she seems at others? Does she find it strange that she has done so many great things on the stage and then finds herself winning an Oscar for an eight-minute bit part in *Shakespeare in Love*? How is she coping without her much-loved late husband, the actor Michael Williams? Does she really hate journalists so much? (A couple of years ago she announced that she would never give another interview.) What is it like to be labelled a great British institution? Does she get tired of all the 'Nothing like a dame' headlines?

As an actor, Dench constantly surprises with the tiniest gestures (a purse of the lips, a flicker of the eyelids, a glance at her loins). She can be matronly and kittenish, severe and tender within the same scene. She often plays peculiarly British women – subdued, judgmental, puritanical, straitlaced, disapproving – and then with one of these tiny gestures she tells us that underneath it all there's something voracious and volcanic and ripe to explode.

She's also a peculiarly British heroine. An underdog. Dench is short and a little dumpy and not obviously glamorous. And yet she can transcend her given lot to become beautiful and heroic. In polls, she is regularly voted Britain's best-dressed woman, Britain's most admired woman (she recently beat the Queen down to number two), the woman we would most like to be.

We've given ourselves plenty of time to get to Cheltenham because the last thing we want to do is be late for Dame Judi. Or so we think. But it slowly dawns on us that we will be late. My friend Helen is driving as fast as she can, but to little avail. Sixty miles to go and one hour to get there. And the traffic is getting thicker and thicker. I phone the press officer at the festival and apologise – we'll be a few minutes late, I say. She sounds stern and disappointed, and says that the whole day has been planned with military precision and there is simply no margin for error. I apologise again. 'You know, Dame Judi hardly ever gives interviews!' she says exasperated. I apologise again. Perhaps if we are late and we can't extend the interview, we could do it on the phone. Desperate situations require desperate measures and the phone it has to be.

(Continued)

'Hello,' Dame Judi says. 'I'm sorry about all this,' I say, 'particularly because I know you give interviews so rarely.' If I'm humble enough, perhaps she'll give me some extra time.

'You do realise that I'm going to come running through into your dressing room any second, panting, tape recorder in hand.'

'That's OK,' she says in that magnificently stripped and clipped voice. 'You're that close?'

'Oh yes, definitely. Possibly closer.' But we're not. 'Are you there, Dame Judi?'

'Yes.' 'Can you tell me what has been the most important book in your life?' 'Most important? No, I don't think I can. But I like books. I like John Fowles very much, though he hasn't written one for a while ...'

'Can you think of a book that has taught you a life lesson?'

'A life lesson. Life lesson? No, I don't think I can,' she says. 'What d'you mean?' 'Erm, I'm not sure. Have you ever chaired a book festival before?' I say, swerving into Helen's lap as she overtakes again.

'No, I haven't. And no, I'm not chairing this one. I'm the president.' Her voice is getting more clipped the longer we talk.

'Yes, that's what I mean,' I burble 'Exactly. President. Are you nervous?' I say, reminding her that within an hour she will be talking to 1,700 people at the biggest books event this country has seen.

'Are you joking?' she says. A refrain I'm to get used to during our exchange.

'Wow! So you're not nervous! Fantastic.'

'Are you joking? Of course I'm nervous.'

It's hard to judge her tone on the phone. I keep getting it wrong. 'You seem to be working so hard since Michael died,' I say. 'There's theatre [she is currently in *All's Well that Ends Well*, although I fear this won't], cinema and presiding over book festivals.'

'Yes, I am working harder since Michael died. You see we always made sure that we made time for each other.'

She and Williams had been married for 30 years when he died of cancer in 2001. He bought her a single rose once a week throughout their marriage. They lived as an extended family in a barn. His parents moved in with them, as did her mother. Does she still live in an extended family? 'Well, they are all dead now,' she says tersely. She stops. 'No, my daughter Finty lives with me, and her son ... ' Family, she says, has always been vitally important to her – when Finty was born she considered giving up work, but Williams told her that full-time motherhood would drive her mad. So she compromised – when Finty was a baby she worked in the theatre in the evening, and when she started school restricted herself to daytime work on television.

Dench has had an extraordinary career in the theatre, playing virtually every female role in Shakespeare. Later, at the talk, she goes through them one by one, dismissing so many performances as failures. She says she botched up Goneril, didn't quite get Imogen, screwed up Regan. Dench is having a harder time with Shakespeare now because there are so few decent

(Continued)

(Continued)

roles for older women. Apparently, when Peter Hall suggested that the time had come for her to play the nurse in Romeo and Juliet she pushed his face into his dinner. Perhaps it's the Irish blood, the passion and spark, that animates the English stoicism. There is another story that once she threw a hot cup of tea at her husband.

'Is it true?'

'Oh, yes. Not just at Michael. But I threw it at my mother-in-law as well.'

'How hot was it?'

'Extremely hot. But it missed them.'

'Blimey,' I say, lost for words. 'Have you ever been arrested?'

'No, I haven't. Well, once I think I was arrested with Vanessa Redgrave at a Ban the Bomb thing. But they let us off because Vanessa had a matinee to do that afternoon.'

Would she say she had a temper? 'Oh, yes. And as I've got older, I've become angrier, more passionate.' She says she's still livid about the war in Iraq. It's funny, I say, how so many men lose their confidence and become enfeebled as they get older, while so many women of a certain age … 'Careful!' she shouts down the phone.

'No seriously,' I say. 'So many women do seem to get stronger and more outspoken the older they become.'

'Well, I think that's a generalisation,' she huffs.

We're still driving in circles. 'Excuse me do you know the way to Cheltenham racecourse?' Helen shouts out to a passer-by.

'Is there somebody in the car with you?' Dench asks.

'Yes, that's Helen,' I say. It feels like a confession. 'I know it seems so intimate, but yes, Helen is here in the car with us.' I think we're finally beginning to hit it off. 'What do you most like about yourself?'

'Erm … ' Silence.

'OK. What do you most dislike about yourself?'

'Oh!' she says, enthusiastically, happier with this question. 'I'm very self-critical. Very. I'm too impulsive. I am too quick to judge people and get things wrong.' She also gets bored very easily, she says. This probably explains why she has done so many different things (from the classics, to sitcoms, to James Bond to working with muscle-man Vin Diesel.)

'What's the best thing about working with Van Diesel?'

'It's Vin Diesel,' she chides. 'Not Van Diesel.'

'Oh sorry,' I say unnerved. 'Van Diesel.'

'No. Vin Diesel.'

'Yes, that's what I mean. Vin Diesel. Is it true he was fighting for you to get paid £4.5 million?'

She burst out laughing. 'Yes, I read that too.'

'And did you get it?'

'Are you joking?'

'What about the half million?'

'Are you joking?'

The trouble with this phone-on-the-road-interview malarkey is that Dench's answers tend to be as staccato as my questions. And when she does answer, I'm so busy diving for cover from oncoming traffic that I forget to follow up.

(Continued)

I promise Dench that we're as good as at the racecourse now. A voice in the background, says that there's only 10 minutes left so I should make the most of it.

'You know you said you had a temper, Judi,' I say.

'No, I didn't. You said I had a temper ...'

'That is very true,' I say. 'I do apologise, it was me who said you had a temper.'

'You concede too easily,' she says.

'I do concede too easily,' I concede. 'And that's a rubbish quality, but in this case I'm conceding because I want to get on to the next question. Is there a new bloke in your life?'

'Are you joking?' she says. 'I'm 69.'

'Well, you're just a baby, so why not, and let's not fall out before we've even met.'

She says something about flattery that I don't quite catch because the wheels are screeching to a stop.

'Guess what,' I say, 'we are finally here.'

I run out of the car, tape recorder in one hand, mobile phone in the other. The same voice in the background says, 'You've got one minute left.'

I run and run, and somehow find myself in Dench's sitting room, panting. She looks smart and sombre in her dark suit and cravat and trademark Joan of Arc crop. I apologise again, tell her how useless I am, ask if there's any possibility of meeting up after the talk. 'No, that will be impossible,' she says.

'Thirty seconds left,' the PR says.

'Dame Judi, could you tell me everything that has been important in your life, everything that has made you happy and made you sad, in the next 30 seconds?'

She looks appalled. 'I couldn't possibly do that in 30 seconds. My family. My family have always been the most important thing in my life, and after that everything is secondary.'

'Time,' the PR says.

'Dame Judi, thank you for the interview.' (Hattenstone 2004)

On other occasions you might be the only journalist – or one of only a few – who wants to do interviews with a particular personality, in which case the chances are that you will be able to set up your own interview at a time and location that suits you better (and a better location might well be the interviewee's own home – see over page).

Whatever the case, watch out for the personality who recounts the same anecdotes and philosophical musings to each journalist they meet. Be aware that many people being profiled tend to rely on the same set of stories and, during the interview, see if you can come up with a new, different or more interesting angle. If nothing else, a novel question, or something not asked before, might help the interviewee to respond more enthusiastically, despite it being near the end of a long and tiring tour that contained countless similar interviews.

David Charters, a feature writer on the *Daily Post* in Liverpool, says you should avoid asking people to tell you anecdotes from their lives:

> You'll end up with something flat. Ask them instead something more general like whether they think table manners are important. It will reveal more. If a person's a bore, write about his dentures or dog instead. Find something unusual about them. Try and get into their bathroom so that you can see whether they are troubled with halitosis, hangovers or athlete's foot. You won't be able to use all the information, but it helps give a more rounded picture. Interviews in the kitchen are better than the lounge. A bottle of Camp Coffee, an Aga, bags of pippins or slippers with the heels flattened at the back will tell you more than any CV prepared by a publicity officer.

PROFILING THE NOT-SO-FAMOUS

Profiles are not just about the famous and wannabe famous. Many newspapers carry features about ordinary people who have done extraordinary things. On the same day that the Norwich-based *Eastern Daily Press* featured a profile of Superman actor Christopher Reeve who had died two days earlier, the regional morning newspaper also ran a feature about four single mums who joined a local community centre to improve their education and turn their lives around. The feature, under the headline 'Mothers given hand to change their lives', highlighted one woman, who had been pregnant and living in fear of drug dealers when she attended the centre, but gained qualifications and was now a trainee outreach support worker.

Feature writer David Bocking specialises in revealing portraits of ordinary people with interesting or unusual obsessions. In his experience, people with a passion, whether it's growing vegetables or collecting 1940s uniforms, provide fascinating copy. 'It seems a bit fey, but I enjoy the opportunity to find stuff out and meet people who do different things.'

SPECIALIST FEATURES

Specialist features concentrate on particular subjects such as health, education, travel, science, local government, the environment or business. They are usually written by a specialist correspondent, although general reporters will also have to write them from time to time. (See Chapter 10 for more on specialist features.)

SPEAKING PERSONALLY ...

... or 'This is what I think' features can be found in just about every newspaper and are the first person 'think' or reaction pieces often written by a journalist or guest writer with a picture byline. They can be serious or funny, caustic or witty, whimsical or straight to the point, depending on the function or purpose of the column, and represent an important part of the overall feature mix: '... one element among many,' says Glover, 'that make a successful newspaper, and if it is removed the recipe will be subtly changed' (Glover 2000: 295).

To some extent, personal columns, and the views expressed in them, are part of a newspaper's personality. Certainly they are one of the very few places where a dialogue is established between reader and writer and, as such, they have an important role in establishing the personality and soul of a paper. The type and scope of personal columns in any publication offer an indication of readership priorities whether it is hobbies (wine, food, DIY, gardening), specialist interests (sport, politics, motoring) or relationships ('At home with H', 'Strictly speaking', 'The kids and I') ... the list is endless.

In regional weeklies and evenings, such columns will often be written by a staff journalist. Larger publications may employ specialist columnists or, increasingly, borrow a celebrity writer from another branch of the media or entertainment industry. The best of these will be well written and well informed with something new and interesting to say. The worst are dreary, self-opinionated rants that are worth neither time nor space. A good columnist, says Ed Guiton, who writes in the *Guardian,* needs to be: 'a good lateral thinker with a facility for encapsulating ideas in simple illustrations that are occasionally amusing'. In other words, writing a good personal column is a hard slog – although we'll provide some tips on how to go about it in Chapter 8.

REVIEWS

Newspapers regularly receive free tickets for Press Nights at local theatres, cinemas and concert halls for the purpose of writing a review about the latest opera, concert, play or musical gig. They also receive copies of CDs and books – and in the case of newspapers with women's interest and/or lifestyle pages, make-up and other beauty products.

Some newspapers do not like accepting such freebies for fear of feeling beholden to the sender, but it is standard practice for the public relations departments of many organisations to offer goodies. However, they should not be seen simply as free gifts or special favours and you certainly must not feel that because you have been given a free ticket to see a show or a copy of the latest crime thriller, that you should write nice things about the show or the book if, in fact, they were awful.

As with any freebie, be honest in your appraisal. The public relations officer of the local theatre who has sent you a ticket to see that week's performance might be disappointed if you write a knocking review, but the chances are that they send out press tickets regularly and are realistic enough and know and understand the rules. See Chapter 9 for more on reviews.

ADVERTORIALS

Increasingly, in an age when advertising revenues rule, journalists are asked to write advertorials. These are articles written in the style of an editorial but paid for by the advertiser. When they appear in a newspaper, they are usually marked as 'advertising' or as a 'special feature'.

You may be asked to write advertorials on a wide range of subjects from kitchen extensions and conservatories to dining room centres and furniture warehouses, and from garden centres and tile warehouses to recruitment agencies and fashion boutiques. You should not feel that, because the feature is being paid for by the advertiser, you must write eulogies. Look on the advertorial as you would any other type of feature and be objective, honest and accurate. Approach it as you would any other feature, that is, look for the best angle, intro and line.

The advertorial is one example where a journalist's copy is sent to the originator for approval. This is because the originator – the advertiser – is paying and wants to amend, comment on or OK the piece. To let anyone outside the newspaper see your copy before it goes to print goes totally against the grain, but a writer of advertorials has to grit their teeth in the face of financial realities. They must also prepare themselves for the fact that the advertiser might want to change the article, adding their own prose, which can often leave the article less than interesting and grammatically incorrect. If this is the case, and you have the opportunity, explain to the advertiser that the original copy was written in an editorial style that fits the tone of the subject and the style of the newspaper in which it is to appear. Be diplomatic.

STYLES

Look through any newspaper and you will see a variety of styles used for features, that is, styles of writing and presentational style. We would suggest, however, that the majority of newspaper features be written in a straightforward way, using plain English to tell simply the story of a person, product or event.

As you become more experienced, you might develop a writing style of your own. Some experienced journalists have done this and their readers have become familiar with it, look out for it and generally enjoy reading it.

> Leeds-based freelance journalist Martin Kelner, who writes a weekly *Guardian* column about sport and television, has a chatty, rather whimsical style that reflects his own slightly ironic take on life. It's hard, he says, to pinpoint precisely what makes a good piece of writing other than a willingness to revise and re-write. He stresses too the importance of intros and endings. 'They're the two key things, although it's nice if there is good stuff in between.'
>
> Sadly, for younger writers, stylish writing tends to come with age and experience, which means, says Ed Guiton, another Northern freelance, that the best advice he can offer is: 'Get older, If you can't do that in a hurry, cut your teeth on something else. Write poetry.'
>
> Put simply, good feature writers are made not born.

Q&A

One favoured style for profiles is the Q&A (question and answer) style, thus:

Q: Should I use a Q&A style here?
A: If it's appropriate.

The Q&A style is where the journalist's questions are marked by a Q, given in full and highlighted in bold, and the interviewee's answers are marked by an A and are also given in full. This style serves the purpose of recounting faithfully either the entire conversation or certainly a large part of it and it leaves the reader in no doubt about what was said. Feature writers sometimes use this style to recount an interview that was long and wide-ranging, and without a particular angle or theme. It might also be used as a way of breaking up an 800-plus word feature into manageable chunks.

You need to think carefully about the questions you are going to ask if you plan to use the Q&A method because this style of feature doesn't allow the use of comment or analysis, observation or colour. The reader has to glean an impression from the questions and answers themselves.

However, if you have no definite angle in mind when you set out to do a particular interview, or you know the interviewee will have a lot of important things to say on a variety of different subjects, the Q&A style might be the one to consider using. Remember, though, that it would still be advisable to edit the piece where appropriate, as not all that is said will be of interest.

ME, ME, ME

Many writers use the first-person style of feature in which he or she makes reference to him or herself in the piece. If you are going to involve yourself in this way, be careful not to use 'I' too often since, as we have mentioned elsewhere, it can start to grate on the reader.

First-person style allows you to make reference, for instance, to how you felt on the day of the interview, how you reached the interview location, and your reaction to what the interviewee was wearing, what he or she said, and what his or her demeanour was. This style allows you to bring in lots of personal observation, but will only be appropriate for those profiles where the character and behaviour of the interviewee, or the particular circumstances surrounding the interview, are all-important.

This style could also be used where the writer is a known name or a local celebrity and considers him or herself as important as the interviewee. First-person features are also widely used by those journalists who want to write about situations and events in which they are very much part of the action.

Younger reporters, hoping to make a name for themselves, particularly enjoy this type of feature. It gives them a chance to face a situation in which they can test their mettle and show off. They might undergo a stunt or a challenge, and then write 800 words recounting their experiences in activities such as parachuting, driving on a skidpan, bungee jumping, learning to ski or taking part in an Army assault course. Gentler activities, but those which lend themselves just as well to the first-person style of writing, include having beauty treatments such as facials, fake tan applications and massages; taking part in chocolate or wine tastings; testing kitchen equipment; employing a personal shopper or wardrobe stylist; and going back to school for the day.

Features of this type are more often than not written in a jaunty, good-humoured manner.

INCLUDING YOU

There are features in which the writer uses the first person and also refers to the reader as 'you'. It is a style that suggests familiarity between the writer and the reader and is often used on newspaper lifestyle and women's interest pages. The writer assumes – often quite correctly – that the reader knows about, and has a joint interest in, the subject being written about.

Exercise

Take a profile feature from a newspaper and reformat it as a Q&A profile. You will need to look particularly carefully at the quotes and think about what questions would have generated those comments.

8 WRITING PERSONAL COLUMNS

The heart of journalism may be news reporting, and the soul of journalism the editorial page, but the personality of journalism is the column.

M. McCabe Cordoza, *You Can Write a Column* (2000: 3)

This chapter:

- looks in more detail at personal columns

- considers what makes a personal column

- examines what a personal column should include.

Personal columns are an integral part of the features mix – they are also, from the point of view of the columnist, one of the most lucrative and satisfying features to write. Financially, a successful personal columnist can expect to earn six-figure sums (at the very least), which is undoubtedly part of the attraction. But for the rest of us, who can only dream of such riches, the lure of column writing is that it offers a stimulating writing challenge as well as an opportunity to let off steam. As Adam Wolstenholme, deputy news editor of the *Spenborough Guardian*, observes:

> There are so many things I enjoy about writing personal columns – the chance to have my own say, the sheer indulgent pleasure of getting something off my chest, or of simply telling an amusing anecdote to make people laugh. But mostly the enjoyment comes from the fact that writing a column feels like *writing* in a way that assembling a hard news story rarely does. It's more playful, artistic, and you have some choice over what you choose to write about.

For a young journalist like Wolstenholme, whose first columns were written for a regional weekly, but who has also had some success writing on a freelance basis for national publications, it can be heady stuff. And, while Wolstenholme, a thoughtful, modest chap, is in little danger of letting his ego get bigger than his byline, it is telling that David Randall in *The Universal Journalist* should write: 'Anyone who has reached the stage of a column either has no need for advice; or has (or will soon acquire) an ego which precludes them from taking any' (Randall 2000: 206). In other words, don't be seduced into thinking that just because you've been given the privilege of your own public soapbox that you've reached a point where you know it all.

All the columnists quoted in these pages emphasised time and again the difficulties inherent in crafting a good column and the importance of revising and re-editing. Freelance Ed Guiton, who wrote his first *Guardian* column in 2004, also acknowledges the contribution of editors and subs, especially in his early days as a columnist when, he says: 'My commissioning editor strengthened my introductory paragraphs if she thought them weak.' Something that now happens 'not too often'.

WHAT IS A PERSONAL COLUMN?

Broadly speaking, personal columns divide into two distinct types:

- **opinion pieces**, which offer a subjective, balanced, rounded view of a current issue or event (and sometimes an individual)
- **personal viewpoint pieces**, which provide an individual slant on a particular topic.

Both are subjective pieces of writing combining evidence, analysis and comment in order to influence a reader's opinion, but there the similarity ends. While a personal column may be an idiosyncratic, bellicose piece of writing that reflects the writer's own viewpoint, the opinion expressed in a newspaper or magazine opinion column is that of the publication and may not necessarily be shared by the individual writer.

Of course, in the nature of things, it is likely that writers will gravitate towards publications that espouse their own particular beliefs on political, social and cultural issues. Nevertheless, there may be occasions when a writer is required to advance an opinion that he or she may not necessarily share – this is not an issue. As David Stephenson points out, 'you are a professional journalist, and there are many shades of opinion' (Stephenson 1998: 102).

Opinion pieces always appear in the same place – in a newspaper on the op ed pages (opposite the editorial or leader) or sometimes on the editorial pages themselves. They will be written either by a senior staff writer or by a guest columnist. (Although these columns usually follow a line determined by the editor or proprietor, occasionally, in the interests of balance, the broadsheet press will recruit a writer from an opposing school of thought to express a contrary opinion.)

The primary purpose of an opinion piece is to leave the reader in absolutely no doubt about what they should think about an issue or event. However, there are differences in the ways in which tabloid and broadsheet or heavyweight publications achieve this aim.

The opinion expressed in the more serious press is implicit rather than explicit – the tone is measured and reasonable. Opposing points of view will be considered and careful arguments will be advanced to explain why they do not stand up. The aim is not to bludgeon the reader but to lead them in a logical way to a reasoned conclusion.

Tabloid opinion pieces, on the other hand, are perfectly happy to bludgeon the reader. Opinion will be directly and forcefully articulated, and the reader will be left in absolutely no doubt that the opinion expressed by the writer is the only possible way for a reasonable individual to think. The regional press tends to fall somewhere between the two – the opinion is more explicitly voiced but the language is more reasonable and moderate than that of the tabloids.

> As a young journalist it is unlikely that you will be asked to write an opinion piece, they are usually the exclusive province of senior, experienced writers. However, should you be given the opportunity, the first step to writing a
>
> *(Continued)*

> *(Continued)*
>
> successful piece is to be absolutely clear what you think about a particular issue or subject. This is one type of writing where you cannot sit on the fence – so make a list of the reasons for or against a particular viewpoint. Says Stephenson (1998: 101): 'This logical process will help you arrive at a sensible conclusion. If you have been told a view to take, do this in reverse order, i.e. conclusion, then your list of reasons. As you will discover, there is an argument to support almost every point of view.'

WORTH THEIR WEIGHT IN GOLD?

Personal viewpoint columns are much more individual in both character and content although they will always have what, in marketing speak, is described as a unique selling point, or USP.

> Ed Guiton says he still finds it strange to be regarded as a professional journalist since his column-writing career is still relatively new. After a long and varied career, he wrote his first column after an accident left him severely paralysed and, initially at least, struggled to adapt his writing style to suit the column format.
>
> I have never studied journalism, nor indeed writing of any sort and I had to convert myself from a writer of reports in local government and voluntary organisations, all of which required very concise writing, to something more discursive. It wasn't easy at first – I tended to pack far too many ideas into each paragraph and write rather elliptically. My first attempts were thrown back at me. My second attempts were more of an historical nature – an account of my accident. These were rejected as being more appropriate to a book, which, incidentally, I am in the process of writing.
> What I was asked to produce were columns of about 800 words based on issues, illustrated by anecdotes and personal experience. I have not always been happy with these constraints. I would like to break out of them – an article on the Paralympics was one such, commissioned at very short notice (about three hours) when I knew virtually nothing about the Paralympic movement.
> I hope to be able to write more about events in the world bringing in my particular viewpoint as a tetraplegic though, truth to tell, I would love to be a political hack.

WHAT MAKES A GOOD PERSONAL COLUMN?

Good columnists have a knack for saying something that sums up perfectly what sensible readers are thinking, even if they didn't know they were thinking it – yet. And they do so, where possible, succinctly and with brevity. So Zoe Williams, in the *Guardian's Weekend* magazine, writing about the Dove 'real women' adverts, says:

> I worked out today why that's so annoying – it's one thing to say 'not all women are thin', but they seem to expect us to be grateful! Like they've won us the vote or something! (Williams 2005)

And it's true – as soon as Williams articulates the thought, what had once been a mildly irritating campaign becomes a seriously patronising bit of marketing. She doesn't mince her words either – getting to the point with a directness and simplicity that, as Carol Sarler (2000) suggests, all journalists would benefit from acquiring. Sarler, who writes for both the broadsheet and tabloid press, reinforces the point with an example from a column she wrote for the *Sunday People* in 1998:

> Much cross-cultural outrage this week at the discovery that Peruvians eat guinea pigs. 'How could they?' came the cry. 'They're so SWEET.' Yes. And lambs aren't? (Sarler in Glover 2000: 252)

No long discourse on the inherent xenophobia of the public reaction; no examination of the cultural, historical, and geographical factors influencing food preferences; no discussion of religious and social taboos surrounding certain foodstuffs. Instead, 30 simple, tightly written words that make the point more effectively than any much longer treatise could have done.

Further, as Sarler (2000: 252) observes, the bonus for the writer is that 'in learning how – when necessary – to condense one's thoughts thus, the pen is all the sharper when writing longer pieces elsewhere'. It is a truth that ought to be more universally acknowledged: writing at length is much easier than writing short. As Guiton admits:

> At first it was difficult but now I find it a help to have a limited number of words. When you are writing to a disciplined pattern it determines the style to some extent. I would have to think more carefully about a 1,500-word column until I got used to it – though the first piece I wrote for the *Guardian* was about 1,500.

And, as he said earlier, was promptly thrown back at him. Good columnists always keep to the specified word count.

WHAT ELSE MAKES A GOOD COLUMNIST?

Lots of things. For starters, meeting deadlines is essential. For someone like Wolstenholme, whose column is just one part of his regular staff job, writing to a deadline is as natural as breathing. Freelance columnists need to be equally meticulous about deadlines and, if they really want to keep on the right side of a commissioning editor, will submit early; furthermore at holiday times, will always have a generic back-up column, on a non-time-critical subject, in reserve.

Good columnists know their audience and their subject – and they never step outside their own field of expertise, although some may stray into slightly different territory for different publications. Zoe Williams, for instance, is, according to Wolstenholme, 'a great exposer of folly and nonsense' and the voice which she adopts in the *Guardian Weekend* magazine is similar to the one she employs in her other life as a columnist for *Now* magazine. But, whereas in the *Guardian*, her column reflects the more middle-class concerns and interests of her readers, her *Now* subject matter is less highbrow in recognition of the fact that different audiences have different needs and expectations.

Finally, good columnists have something to say. The best, most effective personal columns are written by well-read, well-informed writers who offer their readers interesting, well-argued opinions and reasoned arguments on matters of interest or on matters that the writer makes interesting. The worst are written by people who believe their idle musings are of major interest when, frankly, they are not.

One such, written by a male writer, whose identity we will protect by calling him 'R' (as in 'Verbal Rambles with R'), started one of his columns by suggesting he was jinxed and based his premise on the fact that he had once ordered a meal in a restaurant that failed to appear. For the next 700 poorly chosen words in badly phrased sentences, he went into extraordinary detail to explain how, many years later, he ordered a takeaway pizza – and it failed to appear, ergo he was jinxed. His pay-off line was: 'I was gobsmacked.' The whole column should have been well written whimsy. But it was naïve and it failed. The reader was left thinking: 'So what?'

Crucially, such writers have forgotten, if they ever knew, that a good column should be readable, interesting and entertaining. More pertinently, perhaps, they have also failed to recognise that such columns have a built-in, best-before-date since, as Stephen Glover observes, readers sooner or later grow tired of too much forced intimacy. Really successful columnists, he says, are those 'who keep at it, ten, twenty, thirty or forty years, write about the external world, though they may allow the reader an occasional glimpse into their own world' (Glover 2000: 290). In other words, it's a bit like washing your dirty underpants in public – only your mother thinks you, or they, can survive the scrutiny.

> Occasionally, says Wolstenholme, as happens sometimes in everyday life, you say something you regret and advance a case that turns out to be misguided:
>
>> Some of my columns in the run-up to the Iraqi war, for instance, were on the hawkish side, citing the human rights issue and the 'genuine' threat posed by Saddam. Later, we saw the Iraqis worse off than when he was in power and the famous weapons of mass destruction have turned out to be non-existent. It's impossible not to feel very wrong, and that's not a nice feeling. There's always that risk when you stick your neck out about something.

A SOAPBOX NOT A MESSAGE BOARD

Avoid using your column as a message board for those you know or to show what a good person/friend/sport you are. One such writer, talking about the courage of a close friend, expressed her love and support to said friend at the end of three succinct paragraphs, but failed to say how or why the friend had been courageous or needed special love and support. 'I'd rather not go into details ... ' she trilled. But what does this tell the reader? What lessons can be learned? What moral has come into play? What is the point of writing such a piece if only to promote yourself?

Such columnists have forgotten the purpose of a personal column. Columnists exist, says Glover, because editors believe readers want help to navigate through the conundrums, personal and political, of the modern world and, ideally, to entertain them too. 'The good ones do that; the bad ones are a waste of time' (Glover 2000: 294).

GOOD COLUMNISTS ARE NEVER SHORT OF IDEAS

Not true, unfortunately. While Wolstenholme says he often has several ideas bubbling away at once, Martin Kelner, whose Monday 'Screenbreak' column has a very specific theme, admits that some weeks are easier than others. 'I'm somewhat restricted by the fact that the USP of the column is that it's about sport on TV. I can't go off on too much of a tangent.' Instead he is restricted by what he has actually watched, which, on a thin week, can sometimes be a bit of a strain.

'It usually hits me about Friday lunchtime – that I've *got* to think of an idea.' At such times, he envies news reporters and conventional feature writers:

They've got a clear starting point or peg. I'm starting completely from scratch – got to get ideas from wherever although at least the column has a clear theme. It's not a Glenda Slag column, which really is plucked out of nowhere. Once it's in and done I love it. But the idea is the real slog.

Wolstenholme, on the other hand, finds he is rarely stumped for an idea although sometimes, he says, he has to look a bit harder. 'If there's nothing in the news, there's probably something you can use from your own life, if not from last week then from childhood, which you can link with an issue of the day.'

David Charters, a feature writer with the *Liverpool Daily Post*, agrees:

Most of my column writing is not topical. A lot of ideas come from thought – thinking about what will interest people. That is the most important thing – is it interesting? If you can't get two full-length columns out of a British plumber calling at your house to carry out a simple task, you shouldn't be in the job.

Train and bus journeys are there for the writer; funerals hum with material – choice of hats, facial expressions, the hymns or pop songs chosen to see the dearly departed through the hatch – it's all there.

Any observation can be made funny or entertaining – remember that few people are privileged enough to see the managing director of a large company applying mascara to his weedy moustache in the executive lavatory.

Adam Wolstenholme agrees that there is always something to say:

A big news story like the Beslan massacre, say, provides obvious material, but also adds the pressure to have a different take on what you know everyone else will be writing about. Sometimes you see this pressure taking a malignant toll, for instance, the journalist who, after the unprecedented 9/11 attacks made silly comparisons with Vietnam.

However, the dominant news story can be a hindrance rather than an inspiration. It's therefore a good idea to have a few things in the bank. For instance, I've got a piece on political correctness waiting to go as soon as the phrase makes a prominent appearance in the media. I had a piece on Maxine Carr that I used recently, which I'd had waiting for a few weeks until there was a fresh item in the news about her.

There are some ideas that can be used at any time that you can dig out for those weeks when you're short on fresh ideas.

An observation that underlines our earlier point about back-up columns.

> Wolstenholme, Kelner and Guiton are all great believers in lists. Guiton keeps a running list of ideas for columns while Kelner suggests: 'Keep your eye on stuff and keep a notebook handy so you can constantly be noting any ideas you have, based on what's in the news and what you can see around you.'

WHAT SHOULD A COLUMN INCLUDE?

Personal columns, like all the other features discussed in these pages, contain a varied mix of description, information, anecdotes ... and everything else mentioned previously. The difference with a personal column is that the balance and weight of the mix will reflect not only the subject and the writer's take on it, but also the type of column, its purpose and function, as well as the writer's individual writing style – punchy, literary, caustic, whimsical ... whatever. Wolstenholme explains:

> Accordingly, some are purely anecdotal (see Robert Crampton in the *Times* magazine on Saturday). Some have a distinct theme that dictates subject matter and/or tone (Zoe Williams, with 'Is it just me ...?' in the *Guardian* magazine). The late, great John Diamond of the *Times* is an example of a general columnist who was suddenly given a big subject to tackle when he contracted throat cancer.
>
> I think some of my strongest columns have emerged from something commonplace that happened that week – a row with my girlfriend, a delayed train – and some of my weakest have been responses to big, complex issues (Iraq).
>
> Howard Jacobson, in the *Independent on Sunday*, is a deeply thoughtful, literary novelist, and that shows in his columns, which can be flights of fancy or existential musings and are nearly always brilliant.
>
> Julie Burchill's columns are usually rancorous tirades of sexual insult and class prejudice, and the effect is often entertaining, if not genuinely insightful or (heaven forbid) logical.
>
> So there is great variety in the options open to you, which is part of the beauty of it, and my advice would be: play to your strengths. None of this means, of course, that you can say what the heck you like – the usual legal constraints apply, as do those of decency – look (if you can bear to) at Kilroy Silk!

WRITING PERSONAL COLUMNS

As with content, the same basic rules apply. Start, as always, by grabbing the reader's attention, as John Diamond does in this extract from one of his last columns for the *Times*, reproduced in his autobiography *C: Because Cowards Get Cancer Too* ...

> I know what I said last week that I wasn't meant to be here today: as we speak I should be back on the ward with the surgeons chasing the cancer further down my neck But as soon as we arrived at the outpatients' clinic we knew it was all up. (Diamond 1999: 253–6)

His chatty, intimate style – and the hint of something terrible to come – grabs the reader by the throat and guarantees their full attention as surely as a fish hook skewers a wriggling salmon.

Next, expand and develop the intro point:

> Normally, and despite BUPA's hefty chequebook, we conduct our clinical meetings in an ordinary white cubicle in the general outpatients' clinic; this time the receptionist gave us a tight smile and said Mr Rhys Evans had asked for us to be shown over to one of the chain-hotel designed consulting rooms in the Marsden's private wing.
>
> You do not ask your patients to be taken to the comfy chairs if you're about to tell them that, after all, the shadow on the scan was a packet of Woodbines left on the machine by one of the cleaners. (ibid.)

Note how the use of the imagery 'chain-designed consulting rooms' and 'a packet of Woodbines left on the machine by one of the cleaners' helps paint a word picture, while the reference to the packet of Woodbines (smoking caused his ill-health in the first place) also adds dramatic irony. Tellingly, too, he does not immediately spit out the bad news, thus adding further to the tension.

The following paragraphs widen the context:

> Accompanying my surgeon were two men I'd not met before: a consultant medical oncologist and his registrar. Standing behind them, looking embarrassed, was a tallish man in hood and gown with a scythe over his shoulder.

The mix of factual detail – 'consultant medical oncologist and his registrar' – and the Grim Reaper image work together to lighten the tone. This is serious but things are not so bad that Diamond can't find time for a joke. This is important – readers, after all, don't want to start the day crying into their cornflakes or blubbing on the commuter train.

Having established a scenario, spell out the problem, issue or concern, tell the reader what is wrong:

> The cancer is in too many places around my throat and neck to warrant any more surgery. I could ask for a second opinion, I suppose, but quite honestly, it's bad enough having one expert tell you you're going to die without bringing in a second to rub it in.

Again, mindful of his readers, who, remember, have been following Diamond's journey with cancer (he resolutely refused to describe it as a fight) for a couple of years and have invested considerable time and emotional energy in his well-being, Diamond's tone is deliberately matter-of-fact.

Once the scale of a problem has been established, offer reassurance, advice or a solution:

> I realised that the reason I don't seem to be going through the standard denial-anger-bargaining with God-acceptance schtick is because that's what I've being doing for the past 20 months or so. As soon as I heard the first diagnosis I heard a death sentence being passed and I suppose I never thought of the various operations and procedures as much more than temporary reprieves.

In other words, it's OK, guys, I'm cool about this. I've come to terms with it and you don't need to worry about me. But, what about the reader, who has just been given the worst possible news? Give them something to do.

> We haven't told the children yet and won't for a while at least and so, if you come across them – and some of you, I know, do – please don't say anything … I'm sure you'll understand if I don't answer all your mail individually from now on.

These are very intimate and inclusive thoughts. Readers, implies Diamond, are both friends and an integral part of his life and that of his family. He appeals for support and understanding before offering further reassurance about how he is dealing with things.

> And so this is how you find me. Not quite waiting to die because … the same rules apply to the foreshortened life as to the one of normal length; just as no well-balanced 45-year-old says 'Why bother going to the movies I'll be dead in 30 years?, so I find that my imminent death doesn't stop me wanting to know what happens at the end of bad detective thrillers …

He is, he says, still the same old John with the same interests and enthusiasms. He hasn't lost his sense of humour either, although he can't resist throwing in the tragic insinuation that at 45 he is too young to die. Finally, though, because negative endings leave a bad taste in the mouth – and nobody reads a columnist who can be relied upon to depress them – the column ends hopefully.

> We have just returned from buying a basket for the spaniel we are due to collect in a couple of days time … a dog is a happy thing, and it will be happy for me for whatever time I've got left and as happy as things can be for the family when I'm gone.

Hopefully, you won't ever be required to write a column with such tragic subject matter but, whatever your subject, if you follow the structure here you won't go far wrong.

Exercise

Have a go at writing your own personal column in 600 words based on your earliest memory. Remember you have to provide details about the memory itself, the people involved, where it happened and when it happened. You should provide insights into you as an individual and show how the memory has affected your life.

(When you have written the piece, go back through it and take out every unnecessary reference to *I*, *me* and *my*.)

WRITING REVIEWS

... all pop criticism – all criticism? – consists of taking either 'It's great' or 'It's crap' and spinning it over 550 words.'

J. Peel, 'Be cheeky tell the truth',
Guardian Stop Press Fact-Pack (1995)

This chapter:

- looks in more detail at the content and structure of reviews
- considers some of the finer points of writing reviews.

Feature writers divide into two distinct groups: those who specialise in particular types or styles of feature writing and those who work in particular areas, or specialisms, and produce a range of profiles, features and opinion pieces within those specialisms. So, at a national level we have people like A.A. Gill from the *Sunday Times*, who writes reviews (restaurant and television), and columnists such as Zoe Williams, who writes for both the *Guardian* and *Now* magazine, as well as people like Lynn Barber of the *Observer* and Simon Hattenstone of the *Guardian*, who provide incisive and insightful profiles of the rich and famous.

Regional newspaper journalists, on the other hand, are rather less likely to specialise in one particular type of writing genre, simply because most papers don't have sufficient staff to allow them to do so. However, many will have dedicated feature departments and many will have a number of specialist writers covering the main specialist areas outlined in Chapter 10. Mark Bradley, editor of the *Wakefield Express*, for instance, assigns a specialist responsibility to even his most junior reporters because he believes it helps them develop both as writers and as news gatherers: 'If they get a good story, they get the praise they deserve, and, if they make a mistake, they get the criticism they need to learn what they need to do in the future.'

Bradley is proud of his mostly young team. Although like many regional weeklies, the focus is on news rather than features, the fact that he encourages reporters to plough their own specialist furrow means they have more opportunities than most to write outside the narrow box of news story writing. One particularly successful initiative in this direction has been the introduction of a *Wakey Wakey* column, where individual reporters are allowed to sound off about their favourite hobbyhorses. Although these can sometimes read as opinionated rants, they often strike a chord with readers, and, the final test of a successful column, often provoke furious responses in the paper's letters page.

Such a tirade awaited one reporter who wrote an impassioned piece about lunchtime queues, in which she suggested that workers like her would waste less of their lunch break queuing if retired people and other non-employed people shopped at other times of the day. As she soon found out, readers disagreed and a number wrote in to complain about what they considered to be a mistaken piece of reasoning. Says Bradley: 'It was the first time we'd had that sort of response to the column, and, while it was a bit difficult for the reporter concerned, it was interesting that after we published a selection of complaints on the letters page, somebody wrote in to endorse everything that had been said in the original column.'

GETTING STARTED AS A FEATURE WRITER

Many young journalists, especially those beginning their careers on a regional weekly, get their first taste for features by writing reviews. If they're lucky, they will get to cover local gigs and write reviews of the latest compact disc releases. If they're unlucky, they will be sent to do the rounds of the local amateur theatrical circuit and will soon know every line of panto perennials such as *'If you're happy and you know it clap your hands ...'* and *'I know a song that will get on your nerves, get on your nerves, get on your nerves ...'* Nevertheless, it's good experience since all reviews have certain elements in common and, whether you're writing about Sir Ian McKellen's Widow Twanky on the London stage, or Joe Bloggs treading the amateur boards at Brighton, the same rules apply.

It is worth looking at these rules in some detail because many specialist features perform the function of a review in the sense that they all deal with the very basic task of helping the reader decide: is this for me? Is this something I'd like to do, see, hear, eat, wear, try out, visit ...?

FIRST THINGS FIRST

All reviewers need to remember three things: first, they must be absolutely clear about what readers expect from a review in terms of length, content, structure, knowledge, understanding and experience. You also need to take account of time constraints – a reader who picks up a copy of the *Metro* newspaper on the 10-minute bus journey into work has less time to read a review than someone on a 40-minute train commute into a big city. Accordingly, *Metro* reviews are short and punchy, designed to provide readers with a quick snapshot of an event or performance. Broadsheet or magazine reviews, on the other hand, are likely to be longer and more detailed, reflecting the fact that readers have more time to read and digest. Note too that readers of a specialist music magazine, for instance, will have a greater level of specialist knowledge about, for instance, opera than a *Metro* reader. So your language, and, in particular, use of technical terms, and the detail and depth of analysis need to reflect these different levels of understanding.

The second point to remember is that most of your readers will never get to taste, wear, hear, see or experience the subject under review. They know it and you know, so, a well-written review, indeed, any feature, should be a seductive piece of writing that stands alone in its own right.

Finally, don't beat about the bush. As Adam Wolstenholme, deputy news editor of the *Spenborough Guardian*, observes, the best reviews focus firmly on the piece under review. 'Sadly, this doesn't always happen. I hate it when the first half of a review is general waffle. A review of a war film should not pontificate at length about why we like war films, but should ask if this is a successful one, and why.'

DO YOU NEED TO BE EXPERT?

The short answer is yes – and no. Clearly, you can't write a credible review about something if you don't have at least some knowledge and understanding about the particular product or performance under review. On the other hand, you don't need to be a guitar virtuoso to recognise that Bruce Springsteen is, to put it mildly, a competent guitarist. Equally, however, some knowledge of the technical skill required to produce an extended guitar riff is likely to enhance one's appreciation. So, lively enthusiasm and interest is at least as valuable as detailed specialist learning.

> Sarah Carey, now with the *Cornish Guardian*, started writing music reviews as a young reporter with the *Batley News* after she convinced her editor it would be a good way to open up the paper to young people. Although not a musician, she doesn't see this as a handicap.
>
>> You don't need to play yourself so much as know whether or not the band can, so, some understanding of technicalities is necessary although I wouldn't necessarily refer to them in a review.
>> You've got to keep an open mind. I always start by reading the bumph that comes with a new CD, although I usually take it with a pinch of salt. You have to give a track a couple of listens, even if it seems appalling, because you might have missed something first time around. Sometimes things grow on you. First time round you might not like it but if you listen again it might become a favourite. You have to clear your mind of preconceptions and prejudices. I always think: 'This might not be my kind of music but it might be really good for someone who is into that kind of thing.'
>> The aim is to try and get across what the buyer would get from a CD if they went out and bought it – essentially to tell them whether it's any good or not. A star rating system is essential – I give good ones five stars and bad ones get one.
>> Occasionally, you can get away with not being sure about something but, generally, if you don't have an opinion, you shouldn't be doing the job.

WHAT SHOULD REVIEWS INCLUDE?

We talked in Chapter 4 about some of the things common to all features. However, reviews, like all forms of specialist writing, have some specific requirements. These are summarised on the next page.

- **Description and information**. Provide detail and facts – describe what you have seen, heard, tasted, experienced. A film review, for instance, about Mike Leigh's 2005 film *Vera Drake* (Bradshaw 2005) includes description and information about:

  — *the film* – 'a masterly movie'; 'heartwrenchingly moving drama'; 'stunningly acted'
  — *the director* – 'Mike Leigh, icy skill belonging to a master of suspense'
  — *the star* – 'Imelda Staunton'; 'picked up an armful of awards for her performance'; 'certainly collect a lot more'
  — *the character* – 'serial killer'; 'her secret life'; 'middle-aged cleaning lady with a hidden existence'
  — *the plot and genre* – 'suspense thriller'; 'drama'; 'hidden existence'; 'post-war London working class'.

Notice here the use of specific terms and phrases – all specialisms use verbal short cuts, such as 'masterly movie' and 'heartwrenchingly moving drama', to give readers cues about the nature, style and content of the product under review. So, food writers talk about 'steaming hot ripe-as-hell red pepper and nippy mint soup with chunks of butter-drenched ciabatta bread' and motoring correspondents write about engine size, performance, gearing, handling and ride, safety, extras, space, boot size and price. As we've said before, keep a notebook and whenever you come across a phrase or description that strikes you as particularly memorable, write it down and use it later to ginger up your own copy.

- **Context**. Explain the plot, setting and character motivation:

  > It is 1950, and Vera is cheerfully getting on with things. She pops in to help neighbours, nurses her elderly mother and looks after the family. But this life co-exists with, to paraphrase another Leigh title, a secret and a lie: something she's kept quiet from everyone, including her loved ones. With her trusty kit-bag of syringe and other assorted implements, Vera has for decades been 'helping out' wretched girls who have 'got themselves into trouble'.

  A succinct summary that tells the reader exactly what is going on.

- **Preconceptions** (if any). What did you or others expect from the film? Did it meet your expectations? In this case, Bradshaw went along expecting a thought-provoking and moving film from an experienced director, whose work is characterised by a certain grittiness and that is exactly what he got:

  > Leigh gives us his trademark scenes showing the customer class: in *Secrets & Lies*, it was Timothy Spall's photographic subjects; in *All or Nothing*, it was his minicab fares. Now it is women about to undergo illegal abortions.

Note how Bradshaw's references to previous Leigh films and his knowledge of his style and technique establish himself as an authoritative voice.

- **First impressions**. What were your thoughts or feelings as the film opened? Bradshaw's review doesn't dwell on his first impressions – perhaps because he is already familiar with Mike Leigh's work, and can assume that his readers are equally familiar with his directorial 'trademarks'. Instead he makes comparisons with other works that have a similar resonance:

    > Vera Drake's overwhelming mood of danger and transgression reminded me of the moment in Michael Powell's *Peeping Tom* when the seedy newsagent and his furtive customer quickly hide the pornography as an innocent girl comes in to buy sweets.

Again, reference to another, much earlier filmmaker reinforces Bradshaw's authority.

- **Establish what the review is about**. Within the first two or three paragraphs, you must identify the film, genre, plot, director, stars, and their characters, and make it clear what you think about them. In other words, is this a review of a good performance or a bad one?

    > *Vera Drake: portrait of a serial killer.* It wouldn't be an entirely inapposite subtitle for this masterly movie. Mike Leigh captures his heroine's secret life, her modus operandi and her final calamity with the icy skill belonging to a master of suspense. It is as gripping and fascinating as the best thriller, as well as being a stunningly acted and heart-wrenchingly moving drama of the post-war London working class. Imelda Staunton has already picked up a handful of awards for her performance as Vera Drake, the middle-aged cleaning lady with a hidden existence. She will certainly collect a whole lot more.

Bradshaw's intro could, if necessary, stand alone as a simple NIB, since it contains everything the reader needs to know to make a judgement about whether this film is worth seeing or not.

- **Anecdotes** (if applicable). In a review, describing or retelling a particularly outstanding (or poor) scene or incident adds weight in terms of allowing readers to judge from the evidence you offer whether your view is credible or not.

    > With a chirpy smile, Vera arrives in their [her clients'] flats, puts the kettle on (for all the world as if she was making a nice cup of tea) and tells them briskly to pop themselves on the bed and take their underwear off.

The anecdote offers a homely, down-to-earth picture of Vera and her customers.

- **Establish authority**. References to other works by the same director (remember film is a director's rather than a writer's medium) and the stars, together with comparisons to similar works by other producers or performers, reassure the reader that you know what you're talking about. Bradshaw does both as we have seen already.
- **Colour and imagery** – quotes, too, if appropriate. Again, descriptive prose 'wretched girls', 'exhausted and despairing married women' and judicious use of colloquial quotes 'they [Vera's customers] will soon get a pain "down below", at which point they should go to the lavatory and "it will come away"' add dramatic impetus to the review as a piece of writing but also give readers a flavour of what the film is about in terms of content and characterisation.
- **Do I like it?** Should you try it? It is important not to sit on the fence. You should never end a review, as did one (nameless) regional newspaper reviewer, by advising readers to go along 'and make up your own minds'. As a reviewer, your job is to be crystal clear about whether or not readers should waste their time, money or energy on a particular product. In this case, Bradshaw leaves the reader in no doubt about his feelings for this film:

    > This could be Mike Leigh's masterpiece: that is, his masterpiece so far, because at 61 years old, he shows every sign of entering a glorious late period of artistry and power.

- **If it's not working, how can it be fixed?** Bradshaw's review is overwhelmingly positive. As he says above, he regards the film as a 'masterpiece' and, as such, it cannot be improved upon. However, where you find something to criticise you should offer solutions: 'it might have been better if …'; 'a little less action and a lot more dialogue might have made the plot easier to follow'; 'director Y might have produced a better film if he had concentrated more of the action on rising star X rather than big shot actor Z who is past his sell-by date'.
- **Where can you find it?** A colleague (OK, one of us) remembers as a (very) young reporter writing a preview piece about an important festival to be held in the grounds of a local hospital. It was a detailed, informative piece that told readers all they could possibly want to know about what was happening on the day, who would be appearing, where the event was taking place and even what time the fun started. Crucially however, it failed to include the small, but significant detail, about the date. Ouch! All reviews should provide readers with basic information about where they can see, buy or sample a product. Sometimes, this information will be contained in the main body of the piece. More usually it will accompany the review as a separate information box or panel at the head or foot of the feature or alongside it.

> The content of the information box or panels will vary according to the product under review. A film review panel, for instance, will usually contain the names of the director and stars; the film's certificate rating; and, often, the running length. Some sort of star rating is a must. Critics hate them, but readers love them – they allow them to make quality comparisons based on previous star-rated reviews.

SOME THINGS TO REMEMBER ABOUT FILM REVIEWS

Perhaps the most important thing to remember is that a bad film, at least in the opinion of a reviewer, is not necessarily a bad thing. The criteria that a reviewer applies to a film are not necessarily the same as those applied by an ordinary cinemagoer. For him, or her, movies represent a form of lightweight escapism. They're not looking for gritty, thought-provoking reality – they've got more than enough of that in real life. Instead, they want something that takes them out of their, mostly, humdrum existence, which explains, perhaps, why films that are panned by the critics regularly make a fortune at the box-office. Don't, however, let this deter you from applying rigorous critical judgements to the films you review. Your readers will quickly learn your particular preferences and passions and will make their own decisions about which films to see based on their interpretation of your assessment. For instance, if you dismiss something as a 'frothy fantasy', they will know it's just the sort of film they would love, and will be heading for the popcorn forthwith. Similarly, recommend a gripping and stimulating drama and they'll stay at home and watch *Coronation Street* instead. It may be galling that you can't educate their taste to appreciate the finer things cinema has to offer, but you're serving a useful function in acting as a barometer of opinion.

> Adam Wolstenholme, deputy news editor of the *Spenborough Guardian*, offers a couple of practical points:
>
> > When reviewing a play, make sure you get a programme of the performance as they're essential for background information, cast listings and so on. If it's a band, get a copy of their set list. You also need to research their recent history. You don't want to complain in your review that the singer was physically stilted on stage, only to discover later that he's just emerged from a coma after a motorcycle crash.

(Continued)

> Knowledge or experience of the craft under review helps, but it's not essential unless you're writing for a specialist publication. If I'm reading the *Guitarist* magazine, I want to think the person reviewing Eric Clapton's latest concert knows what sort of guitar he's using. A review of the same performance in *The Times* wouldn't require the same level of expertise.
>
> I would say that *some* knowledge or experience is fairly essential for any criticism to be detailed and specific. It's not good enough to say a film had all the ingredients but was 'strangely unmoving'. You owe it to the readers, and the film-makers, to say why it didn't work.
>
> It's also worth mentioning how well a film succeeds *on its own terms*. It's not fair to complain that something on a shoe-string budget lacked gigantic special effects.
>
> Historical context of some films or plays is essential. The internet's very handy for this.
>
> With a film or play, I scribble the odd line of dialogue, or a brief phrase that occurs to me, but generally I don't take too many notes, as it detracts from the performance.

SOME THINGS TO REMEMBER ...

WRITING ABOUT FILM

It might seem fairly obvious but always check your facts – writing about a film, for instance, make sure you get the title right: *Secrets & Lies*, not Secrets and Lies. Spell the names of directors and stars correctly. And if you include a quote from the film, make sure it is accurate. Use an actor's name when discussing his or her performance; refer to the character when discussing the plot.

Although detailed technical knowledge about sound, lighting and photography is unnecessary, don't forget that all three elements contribute to the overall product and may merit comment. Music too helps establish mood and enhances drama so, again, must be considered as part of the mix. Remember, too, that if you mention music and camerawork or any other technical aspects of the film, you *must* credit the individual responsible.

Finally, and this might seem like stating the obvious, film is a visual medium so be aware of the way in which directors use imagery and symbolism to move meaning along. The late, great, movie director John Ford, for instance, was renowned for his use of framing devices to suggest the way his characters were constrained by convention, prejudices and circumstances.

WRITING ABOUT THE THEATRE

As with film, you must identify the genre and outline the plot. Always bear in mind that performances tend to get more polished over time. Take into account opening night nerves, for instance. Because theatre productions are live events, consider audience reactions. Critics were not particularly enamoured of Victoria Wood's 2005 production of *Acorn Antiques*, but almost every reviewer commented on the standing ovation the show received from delighted audiences. Use the present tense if performances are still taking place, the past tense if a run has ended.

Make sure you check for any last-minute cast changes and, as always, if naming names spell them correctly. Don't forget the people behind the scenes – the director, lighting technicians, prop and costume managers. Their efforts, and that of other behind the scenes people, such as musicians, contribute to the overall look and feel of the piece and should be credited accordingly.

WRITING ABOUT TELEVISION AND RADIO

Again, the same general rules apply, although it is worth bearing in mind that neither television nor radio reviews have quite the same weight and authority as, for example, a film review. Both are more transient media and viewers and listeners, in the comfort of their own living rooms, or stuck behind the driving wheel of a car, rarely accord them the same focused attention they apply to something on the cinema screen or stage.

Remember too that although it might sometimes seem as if our TV screens are filled with nothing but repeats, in general, if a viewer doesn't see, for instance, a TV drama the first time it is aired, they are never going to see it. On the other hand, miss a film and you can always catch it on video or DVD later. This means, that it is even more important that a TV review should stand alone as a piece of writing and, perhaps, explains the modern trend (pioneered by Clive James) for reviewers to adopt a caustic, witty, rather world-wearily detached voice.

Three further points. Although a TV drama may be the cinema equivalent of a feature film, in terms of artistic weight and values, those on commercial channels will be subject to frequent advertising breaks. Although reviewers never comment on this, you need to be aware that TV dramatists will have built in dramatic highs or hooks to keep viewers tuned in. How do these affect pace? And do these artificial highs affect narrative flow? Both factors that need to be borne in mind by a reviewer.

Second, reviews will, at reasonably regular intervals, focus on TV soaps, often at moments of dramatic tension – usually births, deaths and marriages. These are tremendously important for viewers – the second wedding of *Coronation Street*'s Ken and Deirdre, for instance, was watched by almost twice as many people as Charles and Camilla's wedding the following day. Whatever your private opinions about soaps, remember that they need to be treated seriously. It is important that you are familiar with plots, back plots and the history of the characters involved. Be aware too that both personalities and plots tend to evolve over time. Les Battersby, for example, was a thuggish loudmouth when he made his *Coronation Street* debut. Several years later, he is still a loudmouth but has now joined the ranks of the Street's comic characters.

Finally, while it is appropriate to take a tongue-in-cheek line with lightweight shows, TV documentaries need to be handled a little more carefully. They are the television equivalent of a well-researched heavyweight feature article, or even a non-fiction book. That means you need to take a more analytical approach to content – think about possible inaccuracies, flawed reasoning and skewed reportage. How sound is the research? What did the director set out to achieve and how well did (s)he achieve it?

WRITING ABOUT BOOKS

It is always a good idea to provide story or plot details early – but be careful not to give away the ending. You must provide brief biographical details about the author in terms of establishing whether this is his or her first book or, perhaps, a follow-up to a surprise bestseller. If it's a first book, can you make comparisons with other writers in the same field? Is the follow-up as good as the original? Use direct quotes from the book to give a flavour of its appeal – or to illustrate the turgid prose. Write in the present tense – books sit around for a very long time. Make sure that you are clear about the author's intention. If the book sets out to be a thriller, does it succeed? It is no good, for instance, complaining, as did one reviewer recently, that a book featuring a family of Ukrainian refugees living in Peterborough, told the reader nothing about life within the town's Ukrainian community. After all, the setting was merely incidental to the plot, which focused on the efforts of two daughters to protect their elderly father from a rapacious second wife. It's a bit like watching a horror movie and complaining that it isn't funny.

Finally, always provide information about price and publisher and, sometimes, number of pages.

WRITING ABOUT FOOD

Describe the décor of the restaurant. What were your first impressions? Did the place live up to your expectations? What sort of food was served – pub grub or nouvelle cuisine? Is it part of a chain or an individually owned establishment? What did you eat? What did your partner or other guests eat? Describe the food, taste and texture, as well as appearance. Did you like it? What did it cost and was it value for money?

Provide some information about the chef and his cooking background. If appropriate, comment on service. Make sure you include information about location and provide details about opening times. It is a good idea too to include a telephone number to make it easy for readers to book a table.

WRITING ABOUT MUSIC AND THE FINE ARTS

Both are non-verbal media, so you must use vivid and pertinent description to explain sights and sounds. References to familiar everyday experiences or incidents often help readers to contexualise something they can neither see nor hear. Jonathan Jones (2000), for instance, writing in the *Guardian*, says that the disciples in Caravaggio's *Supper at Emmaus* register their realisation that their companion is the risen Lord 'not by going down on their knees, but with the kind of stupid, stunned gestures that people might make seeing a goal on TV – pure physical shock'. It is an instantly recognisable picture that enables readers to visualise for themselves the Renaissance masterpiece.

Again, you need to have some awareness or understanding of what the composer or artist wants to achieve. Often, in fact, you will be required to act as an interpreter, explaining and contextualising the work within a larger framework. What sort of emotions does the music seek to arouse? Does it succeed and if not, why not? How does it achieve the desired effect? How does the performance or the performer enhance or detract from the intentions of the creator. Again, consider audience reactions – what was their response to the performance?

It is also important to bear in mind that you will often be writing for a minority audience with substantial knowledge, understanding and experience. Your language and analysis should reflect that expertise.

EXPRESSING YOUR OPINIONS

Don't baldly state that a book, play or meal is good or bad but offer hard evidence in terms of describing something that works – or doesn't, as the case may be. Avoid meaningless adjectives – how tasty is tasty? And don't keep repeating 'in my view', 'I think', 'I feel'. A review, almost by definition, reflects your opinion, your thoughts and your feelings so avoid unnecessary, tautological repetition.

DON'T ...

Go over the top with praise. A measured, balanced, considered review carries more weight than an over-the-top paean of rapture. Never leave before the end (although it's a good idea to sit at the end of a row so you can beat the crowds). And, finally, be careful not to say anything libellous. Criticise the performance and not the performer; the book and not the writer; and the music, not the musician.

WRITING REVIEWS: THE RULES

The rules for writing a review are the same as for any other type of story. Essentially, says Wolstenholme, a review has two purposes. 'It should do justice to the work of art in question and produce an entertaining piece of writing. If possible, do both simultaneously.' In other words, you need to write an intro that grabs the attention and the piece should be informative and/or entertaining and all the facts should be correct.

In writing a review of a play, film or book, avoid giving away the whole story. The temptation for a journalist new to writing reviews is simply to recount what happens in a '... he did this, then she did that and then this happened ...' sort of way. Certainly you should give a flavour such as: 'The action is set in the deep south at the height of summer when not just the temperature but tempers too were simmering ...' However, rather than detail specifics, try hinting: 'We get a sense in this play that not everyone is being as honest as they could be. The ending comes as something of a surprise when we realise exactly who has been doing the double-dealing.' Which is better than revealing all and thus spoiling the reader's enjoyment by giving away too many details, too much of the action – and the ending.

Tell the reader what you liked or disliked about the item or event being reviewed – and explain why. It is not enough to say: 'The play was rubbish from start to finish ...' as this doesn't tell the reader why you think this and doesn't take into account the fact that one person's rubbish is another person's art. If you are going to be critical during a review, be sure you can justify your censure, explain or argue the case well and make sure you do not libel anyone.

In his review of a Bill Wyman concert for the *Hull Daily Mail*, feature writer David Clensy manages to capture the atmosphere of both the evening and the personality of the musician in a piece that is written in a lively style, which sets the scene and describes the action, leaving the reader with a sense of what it must have felt like to be there:

> The Rolling Stone who rolled away, landed up in Hull City Hall last night and brought the house down with his all-star Rhythm Kings band.
>
> He may be pushing three-score years and 10, but the legendary bassist Bill Wyman proved he can still put on a show, just a couple of weeks after announcing this will be his last tour.
>
> It's hard to put a label on the Rhythm Kings' show (perhaps that's the idea). To call it simply a rock 'n' roll show would somehow be missing the point – and failing to acknowledge the wonderful swathes of blues, rhythm and blues, boogie-woogie and soul that kept the show constantly changing gear.
>
> But the evening opened with a definite rock 'n' roll feel – a vibe which culminated in Mike Sanchez's slightly manic rendition of That's Alright Mama.
>
> With great singers like Sanchez in the line-up, there's really no need for Wyman to break from his familiar 'I'm bored-stiff with life' bass-playing pose.
>
> But he did step up to the microphone for one song last night, a slightly tongue in cheek performance of C'est La Vie Said The Old Folks. It goes to show you never can tell – bass players, even Wyman, can occasionally crack a smile.
>
> Wyman's clearly proud of the band he's formed around him since breaking with the Stones 11 years ago.
>
> He introduced each member like a proud father-figure last night (a fag hanging limply from his mouth at the time).
>
> The incredibly talented Albert Lee, he dubbed 'the guitarists' guitarist', Terry Taylor, he said was his 'best friend ever', and Mike Sanchez, he mused, was an (expletive deleted) 'idiot from Kidderminster'. But there was real affection in his voice as he said it.
>
> And Bill had a surprise guest up his sleeve (well, in the wings to be precise). The iconic voice of Eddie 'Soul Man' Floyd really got the audience to their feet, as he belted out his classic hit Soul Man, followed by a flurry of familiar soul numbers.
>
> After a brief encore the band left the stage to a standing ovation. Just a few more gigs then, and Bill can finally start gathering some moss.

Don't feel guilty about criticising a poor performance. Says Wolstenholme: 'Poor performances need and deserve to be slagged off for the sake of the wider culture. But poor reviews shouldn't be gratuitously cruel. Slagging off a good performance – that's something to feel guilty about.'

Exercise

Select a film review, book review and a music review. Go through and identify the cue words that provide information about the performance under review.

Now, write a review of a recent TV programme, film, book or CD, incorporating as many of the significant cue words as possible.

10
SPECIALIST FEATURES

If you're passionate about something your enthusiasm will show in your writing – but enthusiasm is not enough. For many topics it is important to have reliable and up-to-date knowledge.

J. Dick, *Freelance Writing for Newspapers* (2003: 51)

This chapter:

- examines in more detail some of the most popular types of feature writing

- looks at specialist feature subjects such as health, business, crime, travel and women's interest

- considers regularly appearing features.

Feature writers are often asked if they have a specialist subject on which they write. Many enjoy writing general features on a wide range of subjects that encompass specialist areas such as health, business or education. Others prefer to immerse themselves in one subject (perhaps something they studied at university, have a natural talent for, or a genuine interest in). They make a speciality of a particular subject and cultivate contacts particular to that specialism.

The nationals and many of the larger local and regional newspapers have specialist writers on their staff. But that is not to say that a specialist writer will work exclusively in their subject area; in fact, we would argue it is a good thing that writers do not become blinkered at the expense of features of a more general nature. On smaller local papers general reporters will find themselves having to write features and these will include specialist features. Some of you might feel unable, ill equipped or uninterested in writing features of a specialist nature, that is, about a specialist subject of which you know nothing, very little and/or have no interest in. However, you will have to find the interest and energy – and become an instant expert in whatever the subject happens to be because some of your readers will have an interest in that area, and your editor has deemed it a subject worth covering. Journalists new to feature writing cannot afford to pick and choose the subjects they write about – in fact, journalists a little longer in the tooth cannot afford to be precious about the subjects they tackle either.

> Nick Morrison, features editor of the *Northern Echo*, says there are ways to use specialists and ways to use general writers to write on specialist subjects:
>
> > For specialist subjects it is very useful to have someone who has a certain level of background knowledge. The other side to this is that it can be useful also to have someone write about a specialist subject they know little about because they will then ask the questions that are needed to explain the subject thoroughly. A specialist might not ask these questions because they might assume a level of specialist knowledge from their readers that isn't there. Having said that, it is good to have specialists who know the right people to go to for information and who can turn a specialist feature round effectively and well.

For a freelance writer to specialise, he or she would need to cultivate a specialist market that would include specialist pages in a national or regional newspaper, or specialist journals and magazines. They would also need to be capable of producing regular features in that subject area. Many freelancers prefer to write general features so that they can write on a wider variety of subjects and spread their wares around a wider marketplace. In the same vein, if you are someone new to writing features, our advice would be to keep it general while trying your hand at the occasional specialist feature.

But remember, even though you are writing on a specialist subject, the same rules of feature writing apply: you need a strong peg and a good angle. Do your research and carry out interviews. Keep the writing simple – and tell the story. The subject might be medical, scientific or technical in nature but this should not be an excuse to litter your copy with words and phrases that are not in everyday use – and, if you have to throw in the occasional medical, scientific or technical term, make sure you explain what it means.

In a sense, says freelance writer Julie Gillin, who specialises in writing about health and travel, the job of the journalist is to act as a translator between expert and reader:

> I find doctors often aren't used to talking in lay terms. So, I start by getting them to explain something as simply as they can; then I get them to explain each part of what they've told me again; each time I'm trying to get them to strip down the layers of technical jargon so that people like me can understand it.
>
> Sometimes, before I go to an expert in a particular field, I'll talk to another doctor with more general experience who will help me to get a handle on a complex subject and help get around the technicalities.

Remember images when you are writing specialist features. They can often be as important as the subject you are writing about and can certainly break up great slabs of text on the page. Images, including pictures, graphics, cartoons and drawings, will generally be used bigger to accompany a specialist feature than they would to accompany a news story.

HEALTH

Health matters offer a huge and fascinating subject area for feature writers – and represent an important and expanding area of journalism. Not only do newspapers and magazines have dedicated health pages – where a doctor might write a regular column on the latest health scare, hospital bug or ground-breaking treatment, while specialist staff writers, and often freelances too, will produce a range of features on health-related or medical matters – but, increasingly, new titles are springing up devoted solely to health issues.

This growth reflects important changes both in the nature of society and in the way we think about health. First, the move away from a social structure based around the extended family means that traditional sources of information (granny, wise women, faith healers) are no longer on hand. As a result, most of us have only a small, inexperienced (at least, in matters of health) circle of intimate and trusted confidants. Second, health deals with big issues affecting people – life and death, sickness and suffering, and medical miracles – all of which feed our voyeuristic instinct towards human drama. The health writer, at different times, fulfils all these needs by providing information, experience and human interest.

Third, as Vivienne Parry (2005) observes in her 'Last word' column in the *Guardian*: 'Though we live longer and are healthier than before, the richer and healthier you get, paradoxically the more likely you are to be unhappy about your health and seek treatment.' In other words, we all enjoy ill health – and, most pertinently of all, we enjoy reading about it.

Broadly speaking, writing about health falls into two distinct categories: the psychological approach and the medical model. The first seeks to address issues around the fact that although our society is materially rich, as individuals we are often poor in terms of personal fulfilment. As a result, we are more likely to be stressed, anxious or suffering from depression than in the past or, alternatively, may find that our psychological malaise is manifesting itself in physical symptoms – eczema, for instance. The role of the health writer here is to offer reassurance and solutions and to encourage readers to feel able to take control of their own health.

The second approach, on the other hand, deals with a medical response to an identified problem and, although the reader should never be blinded by science, the focus will often be on the importance of medical breakthroughs in terms of improving quality of life. Of course, the two approaches may not be mutually exclusive – an in-depth health piece, for example, would typically combine the two, including information about new medical treatments with an inspiring case study about an individual's positive outlook in the face of a debilitating or life-threatening illness. A personal column, however, would tend to focus on one aspect or the other. Dr Thomas Stuttaford in the *Times*, for instance, is a good example of the medical model, while the *Observer's* Barefoot Doctor tends towards the psychological approach.

FIRE-FIGHTING – AND HONESTY

While news health stories are time-specific and generally linked to an announcement of a new treatment or other medical breakthrough, health features are not necessarily so strictly timed unless they are linked to a particular health awareness week, for example.

Needless to say, a health writer needs excellent contacts that include doctors, nurses, hospital staff and those working for the various health organisations such as primary care trusts.

More importantly, though, and this, perhaps, applies to health more than any other specialism, health writers *must* take a responsible attitude to the information they put into the public domain. Says Julie Gillin:

> Health is an amazing area. A lot of it is fire-fighting – things like the bed crisis. But as well as big things like research or equipment, there is a lot of human life and interest. You're dealing with important issues and, if, for instance, you're talking about something like cancer, you've got to be really honest. People sometimes suggest there's a cure around the corner, and there might be, but, equally, it might be a generation away or five years away, and that's too late for some people. But you've got to tell it like it is because it's not right to raise false hopes or expectations.
>
> You've got to be careful, therefore, to get the science right and, although, I know the general rule is not to go back and let people read your copy, if it's technical, I prefer to get it checked.

TYPES OF HEALTH FEATURE

Where some specialisms (politics and business, come to mind) are almost unrelentingly serious and sober, health journalism covers a rewarding mix of soft and hard news stories or features. Typically, health features might be:

- **product review**: e.g. how to choose a gym to suit our lifestyle, slimming aids, new types of cosmetic surgery
- **health news**: reports, scare stories, medical breakthroughs
- **common or unusual ailments**: e.g. a new product or treatment for the common cold or a human interest story about someone living with a rare disease or condition
- **aspirational feature**: e.g. follow this diet and you too can lose seven pounds in seven days
- **human interest**: stories that leave the reader thinking either 'Thank heavens, that's not me', as in 'I lost both my legs in a car crash', or 'How did she cope?', as in 'My baby weighed less than a bag of sugar at birth', in either case the focus is on a special individual who has faced insurmountable odds.

> Journalist Kate Lahive, health correspondent for the *Sheffield Star*, loves the variety and creativity of health journalism:
>
> For example, a recent feature I've written about childhood obesity started with a poem by a young teenager which expressed her conflicting feelings about battling her weight problem. And I think it worked – as it gave an insight into her feelings and the piece that followed looked at the complex psychological reasons that drive youngsters to over-eat.

COMMON ELEMENTS OF HEALTH FEATURES

All health features should include:

- information about the condition – its prevalence, symptoms, outcomes
- treatments – whether medical or home remedies
- case study – based on an interview with someone affected by the particular issue
- expert view – a doctor, nurse or therapist (although never rely on just one source).

STRUCTURING A HEALTH FEATURE

Health writing follows the same broad structural rules established earlier – that is, lead with the strongest point; establish early what the feature is about; keep the focus on the individual involved but make sure you explain the wider context; and use quotes, case studies and experts to provide insights and evaluation.

Remember, too, what we said in Chapter 4 about different authorial voices. Be clear about which voice you are adopting and be careful not to patronise your reader, especially when explaining or summarising complex medical terms or phrases. Address the reader as an equal adult or friend.

Endings should refer back to the opening paragraph – although don't simply restate or repeat it. Instead, consider offering a personal view or judgement; or, perhaps, provide the reader with a food-for-thought idea or a suggestion for future action. Don't leave the reader feeling negative or depressed. Always end with something positive or optimistic.

> Kate Lahive of the *Sheffield Star* stresses the importance of the human interest element:
>
> Ideally I'd aim to explain the impact of a complex health procedure through the experience of a patient. A recent story I did was about a woman who had brain surgery while wide-awake, and strapped to the operating table, to quell the shakes she was experiencing from having Parkinson's Disease.
> It was very interesting as she explained the personal side of things (i.e. what it was like having brain surgery while conscious), what life had been like before the operation and how it was much better since. There was quite a complex medical side from the doctor's point of view, and I also wanted to explore this side of things, and hopefully was able to translate this into something that was clear and understandable.

> *(Continued)*
>
> I also included a fact file on Parkinson's Disease – to give people an insight into the condition – which is something I would aim to do in most health features in order to give readers extra information that doesn't fit into the main body of the story.

BUSINESS

Business writing, as with any other form of specialist writing, must follow the general rules of feature writing. Work on the basis that even though you are writing about business, the story is the story, and that goes whether what you are writing about is a small one-man business in Bognor about to go bust or a multinational organisation making millions of pounds in profits. Look for the peg; find a good angle; get your facts (and figures) right – and tell the story.

Sion Barry, business editor of the *Western Mail*, says there is little difference between general news and business news: 'If a man falls off a bridge and dies, you know that is the line. So, if a company loses a major order, that's the line. You have to tell the story; get the key facts across. Even though the content is different, the discipline is the same.' And when it comes to writing business features, the recipe is the same as with general features too:

> With business news there is a lot of factual information you must get across but with a feature – although you must still get your facts in and get them right – you can bring in human interest and colour too. For instance, if I was writing about a company in Wales that had won a major new contract, that would be the news story. But I might write a feature about the chief executive of the company to add a more personal dimension. I'd ask general questions about his private life; how he got involved in the business; how he spends the time when he's not at work; what makes him tick – that sort of thing.
>
> I try to make all my business stories lively, but with features you can bring in extra personality and colour.

CRIME

Chris Greenwood, assistant news editor on the *York Evening Press*, joined the paper as a trainee reporter, eventually becoming crime reporter when a vacancy arose.

> I always loved chasing news and it was natural to move into crime where I could chase people, work on things that were happening now, knock on doors and solve problems.

Because of the nature of crime stories, you need a strong stomach and, to an extent, you get hardened to situations. But you can also run the risk of sensationalising. You must always remember the reader and consider what you are going to write and how that will affect them. For instance, in a double murder case I covered, the victims' bodies were left to decompose by a radiator and when police found them they were literally falling to pieces. How much of that can you write? How graphic can you be? You can't wrap the reader up in cotton wool to protect them but you have to find a way to report the facts as honestly as you can without offending or upsetting anyone.

Although I love the chase of news stories, I also enjoy writing news analysis features. I try to get reporting into them by putting in new information. Some feature writing is just hashing together stuff that is already in the public domain, but I try to get a new angle and include new information.

A specialist writer comes into his or her own when the news desk wants an in-depth analysis of a particular story. For instance, we were running a story about gun crime and I was asked to write a feature looking at gun culture. I already had a lot of background knowledge in my mind and I had contacts I could turn to – I had their mobile phone numbers and I had spoken to them before and they are comfortable with me. On this occasion I got some more background information from a source who works in the police force but, because he was quite junior, I grabbed a more senior officer to get him to substantiate what I had been told.

Here we reproduce the feature, published in the *York Evening Press* (11 April 2004), which Greenwood uses to offer an analysis of, and background to, the growing trend in gun crime. He also highlights the work of armed police officers who have to deal with gun crime. He is able to include extra information that would be too much for a punchy news story, but adds valuable reporting; and to use a style of writing that would not be as appropriate for news.

It's the trouble with guns

It's late on a Friday night and a police 999 operator receives a report that a man is drunk or high on drugs and is shouting abuse at people in the street. Perhaps this is not an unusual event, but this incident has extra urgency – a bystander says he is carrying a gun.

Before police can be sent to the scene, senior officers must judge what danger they face. They ask themselves a series of questions. Is the information credible? Who is the assailant? Does he have a history of violence or access to weapons? Intelligence gathered on police databases can help, but all officers are eventually left with a judgment call.

The authorising officer will deploy firearms if he has reason to suppose that his men may be confronted by an armed individual, someone who has access to weapons or who is otherwise so dangerous that the officer's use of a firearm may be necessary.

(Continued)

His firearms team are highly trained people who have been selected for their abilities in planning and restraint as well as emotional strength, alertness and, crucially, decision-making under pressure. If they confront the man and he points the gun at them, they may be called to make a split-second life and death decision. It's a job few would envy.

The tragic reality of the role of the police marksman has been thrown into sharp relief by the recent suspension of two Metropolitan Police officers after a second inquest into the death of Harry Stanley, 46, returned a verdict of unlawful killing.

The two officers shot him dead in Hackney, East London, in 1999, after confronting him near a pub where he had been drinking. They thought he was pointing a shotgun at them, but in fact the 'gun' was a table leg, which he had recently repaired and placed in a bag.

Up to 125 armed officers went on an unofficial 'sympathy strike' in the capital when they learned of the men's suspension and Sir John Stevens, the most senior police officer in the country, called for more legal protection for the 'difficult job' firearms specialists carry out. The strike was called off yesterday after talks.

In North Yorkshire senior officers have invested heavily in our own armed response capability. Although the number of criminals who possess guns in the county is relatively low, the force is prepared for any eventuality. Last year 135 firearms incidents took place in North Yorkshire, a tenth of the 1,300 that occurred in West Yorkshire.

Armed officers are also deployed to protect the two controversial military bases at Menwith Hill and Fylingdales, which are seen as potential terrorist targets, as well as protecting royal visitors and VIPs. The officers are also tasked to take part in day-to-day operations which may target trouble hotspots or places hit by vehicle crime.

A new purpose-built facility for armed officers will soon be unveiled at Thirsk and officers are this week moving their equipment from Easingwold. The newly formed Firearms Support Unit, led by Inspector Richard Armstrong, will then operate from Thirsk and Tadcaster.

Inspector Armstrong recently told the *Evening Press* that the 100-strong North Yorkshire Police unit was better prepared than ever to deal with a terrorist attack or terrifying armed incident and that he is confident in the ability of his officers to protect the public.

Chief Superintendent Tim Madgwick, York and Selby area commander, led the armed siege which took place off Windmill Lane, Heslington, York, earlier this week when the police received a report that a man was inside his house with a pistol. He successfully defused the situation and resident David Roustoby gave himself up.

Mr Madgwick said he cannot comment on the operation because talks are ongoing with the Crown Prosecution Service as to whether charges will be brought against Mr Roustoby, and police weapons experts have not completed their analysis of a handgun found at the scene.

But the senior officer has added his influential voice to a growing chorus calling for a ban on replica firearms. He points to a series of incidents in the city when officers carrying deadly weapons were brought in because someone was playing with a realistic-looking toy.

(Continued)

(Continued)

One such incident took place at Burton Croft, in Clifton, when a security guard reported he had seen a gun lying on the floor of the disused nursing home after it was occupied by squatters. It later proved to be a toy pistol. In another case armed officers were called to Garfield Terrace, off Leeman Road, as they attempted to arrest an armed robber who threatened post office staff with a six-inch metal cylinder.

In both incidents police said that there were no 'half measures' when there was a chance that officers could be confronted by a firearm. In neither incident was a real gun found.

Mr Madgwick said: 'There are too many of these things around. It is impossible to tell them apart from the real thing, especially in the dark or when they are being waved around. I would fully support a ban on the sale of replica firearms.

'They are either used by criminals to commit robberies or other things because they have got no legal use. Even when they are in the hands of ordinary people who are interested in firearms they can cause problems.

'As a senior officer, if I put my officers in a situation where they have reason to believe there is a firearm I have to respond at the appropriate level.'

But gun enthusiasts say they are living within the law and said a blanket ban would create even more problems. Even then, Stuart Sykes, of Blue Moon Trading, which stocks such replicas, said he did not envy the police's job.

He said: 'It's a difficult situation. The police have a vested interest in saying that. It's the same as a vegetarian wanting the law to ban butchers' shops.

'I'd love to live in a perfect world but you can't legislate against fools. Nearly every month some fool acts silly with something. There are a lot of problems with alcohol in this country but there's no point in closing all the pubs.'

He added that the debate on replica weapons and air guns had gone on for 40 years and would rumble on for another 40.

He said the 'ban it all brigade' did not provide the answer. 'It didn't work with drink and guns in some parts of America', he said.

Mr Sykes said part of the problem stemmed from magistrates not handing down tough enough sentences to people caught misusing air guns. 'We have police officers who are customers and they say the same thing,' the shop boss said.

'Put these people in front of the magistrates and (because of the sentences they receive) they come out laughing and they do not give a damn. This is not sending out any kind of warning.' (Greenwood 2004)

Greenwood's feature was accompanied by pictures of replica firearms; a police negotiator during a five-hour siege at a house where the occupant was believed to have a gun; Chief Superintendent Tim Madgwick, one of the interviewees; and the scene at another house where it was believed an armed robber was hiding out. A separate box contained pictures and details of other gun incidents in the area.

THE TROUBLE WITH GUNS: AN ANALYSIS

Look at the intro – which we saw previously in Chapter 6 – and consider the use of the interesting narrative style that draws the reader in and then follows up with a punch in the final eight words.

The second paragraph offers an insider's view into how the police are thinking. This information has obviously come from Greenwood's sources, but is not directly attributed as it might be in a news story. Here, facts accrued are presented by way of the writer's own questioning.

The fourth paragraph includes details about the firearm's team, which, in a news story would be presented in a concise way: 'the highly trained, alert firearms team' for example, but here, Greenwood is able to elaborate. Drama is added in the second sentence, and the third sentence, although offered in a matter-of-fact tone, also adds drama.

The fifth, sixth and seventh paragraphs offer news background on a firearms case, which gives the feature a meaty reason for being – especially since it is linked topically to something that happened 'yesterday'. It not only gives facts but puts into perspective the very real 'life or death' decisions that officers must make and which Greenwood referred to earlier. It could also be seen as empathising with the officers, showing them in a personal, human light.

Paragraphs eight and nine reintroduce local interest – offering facts and figures of specific interest to readers in the region, while the tenth paragraph offers another strong news peg.

Paragraph 11 introduces Inspector Richard Armstrong who is quoted indirectly; his comments having come from an earlier interview and probably used in an earlier news story. Paragraph 12 brings in Chief Superintendent Tim Madgwick and another strong, topical news peg – the incident that happened 'earlier this week'.

Paragraph 15 offers background on previous firearms incidents, which Greenwood has either taken from the cuttings, or, if the incidents have not been covered as news stories, have come from Greenwood's police sources.

Paragraph 17 offers a strong news angle to the feature.

Paragraph 20 to the end introduces the alternative view, that of gun enthusiast Stuart Sykes – perhaps one of Greenwood's sources already, given his interest, but certainly someone Greenwood has interviewed. Sykes has a different perspective to the police on the ownership of replica guns and offers a balance to what has gone before.

TRAVEL FEATURES

Journalists receive a number of perks, which can include free travel and holidays. Some journalists refuse to accept these on the grounds that they are not to be bought or persuaded by organisations hoping for free and positive publicity. Our view is that perks, or freebies as they are also known, are an accepted part of the industry and, as long as the system is not abused and your newspaper allows you to take up such offers, there is nothing wrong in accepting them.

Remember though, you must not feel under any obligation to write a glowing eulogy about the travel company and/or holiday hotel, nor can you guarantee that whatever article you write will be published (that decision lies with your editor). But if you accept a free offer and write about it in the same way you would any other feature, that is, truthfully and in a fair and balanced way, we cannot see anything wrong with the practice. Used well by accredited journalists, tickets for free flights and holidays can lead to informative and entertaining features that highlight and expose destinations, warts and all.

There is also the opportunity to turn your own paid-for holidays into features.

TWO TYPES OF TRAVEL FEATURE

Julie Gillin, who specialises in both health and travel writing, divides travel features into two distinct categories. The first is the rather esoteric, aspirational feature that tends to appear in the broadsheets or heavyweight press – features about exotic (and expensive) holidays in out-of-the-way places that we might daydream about visiting but which, realistically, are beyond our pocket and our reach. 'It tends to be a more creative type of writing. The aim is to give the reader a "feel" for a place, a taste of what they might experience if they ever make it there', says Gillin.

The second, rather more common, type of travel writing is more down-to-earth. The emphasis is less on the gorgeousness of the place and rather more on its suitability as a holiday destination for a working family that can afford one decent break a year. As Gillin explains:

> The bottom line is that they [readers] want to know whether they'll get value-for-money and whether the kids are going to have a good time. The children are particularly important. For most families, if the kids have a good holiday, the parents do too. So you have to be honest – you've got to tell them whether a hotel is in a noisy part of town and the kids won't be able to sleep.

She recalls one holiday some years ago when her daughter was still a baby and the travel company arranged a hire car for Gillin and her husband.

> They were extremely helpful and made sure there was a car seat in the front for my little girl. But it wasn't until after we'd set off that we realised that the car was fitted

with air bags and that they shouldn't have put the baby seat on the front passenger seat.

I suppose it was our mistake too, but as a company they shouldn't have been providing customers with that particular type of car seat. So, we had to go back to them and point out that it was something they needed to sort out.

They were very apologetic and, rather than slagging them off about it, I included a fact file that warned holidaymakers what to look out for.

While she admits that writing about travel has resulted in more and better holidays than she might otherwise have afforded – 'We always get the best accommodation and treatment' – it does mean that holidays are rarely completely relaxing. 'I don't go away with pen and paper in one hand,' Gillin says, 'but I'm always thinking: "Could I say to another family, you could come here?" It's usually a couple of days into a holiday – when I know I've got what I need to write a piece when I come home – that I can begin to unwind.'

Travel pieces should always include details about cost, location, how you got there and how long it took. If possible, include illuminating anecdotes and an honest assessment of the accommodation and the resort.

WOMEN ONLY

Women's pages come in all shapes and sizes – from a one-page special tucked away towards the back of the newspaper to an eight-page supplement produced on a particular day of the week. Traditionally known as the women's pages, they are now more likely to be called lifestyle pages, encompassing as they do subjects that include wider home, family and entertainment matters.

Writers working on these pages should remember their audience and the subject matter and choose their style accordingly. Generally, the writing style and layout will be lighter and brighter in tone than for, say, the business pages, but this is not to conclude that women's pages are all froth and gloss – far from it. They carry a variety of features that span a diverse range from human drama and misery to the latest in lip-liners and summer sandals. And a woman's page writer must reflect the subject matter in his or her writing.

On a broadsheet lifestyle page, for instance, they might use a bright and breezy style of writing to describe a new fashion trend while taking a softer tone to write about someone's medical condition and a more matter-of-fact technique to offer information in a side panel about, say, natural remedies.

> Susie Weldon, woman's editor at the *Western Daily Press*, covers a range of issues from health to beauty to fashion to human interest:
>
> I always like to feature women in our area who are doing interesting things. These are quite often 'soft' – for instance, a story about two women running marathons in coming months, one in the Sahara and one at the North Pole; the woman who has set up a business selling items on eBay; the Bristol women whose lingerie designs sell in top stores around the world. But we also cover 'harder' women's issues such as rape; mothers jailed after wrongly being convicted for murdering their babies; and ordinary people dealing with extraordinary difficulties or trauma in their lives and turning a tragedy into a kind of triumph – a triumph of the spirit, that is.
>
> With style, we can be far less formulaic in our writing than in news; more informal perhaps or more quirky, but always focusing on the human element of the story. We're more descriptive, use much more colour and occasionally (but not too often) will inject our own observations into the piece, unlike the news reporter who must maintain an anonymous presence.
>
> The reason why I love working on the women's pages is the huge mix of topics. One moment I'm being wrapped in mud bandages because I'm trying out some beauty therapy, the next I'm interviewing a mother whose four-month-old daughter came down with meningitis and only survived after having both her legs and one arm amputated. And she's telling me how her severely brain-damaged daughter, now aged eight, has taught her about love, compassion and the true value of things in life.
>
> A lot of hard news types think the women's/lifestyle pages are frivolous and, yes, the best of them are – we all need a bit of frivolity to lift our spirits at times. But they also deal in real lives and real emotions in a way that doesn't always come through in news unless there's been an atrocity, disaster or murder somewhere.
>
> I truly believe that the women's/lifestyle pages can help knit communities together – certainly on a regional or local paper – because they give space to ordinary people and their often eccentric, amusing and, frankly, odd ways.

THE REGULARS

Regular niche columns written by specialist and/or guest writers are many and various. They include articles on wine, alternative health, walking, bird watching, chess, bridge and so on. Nick Morrison says columns such as these in the *Northern Echo* are usually about 200 words long and appear on a regular weekly basis:

> A lot of them have been running for a long time, and are written by guest writers who have been doing it for years. They fulfil an important role. They appeal to a minority of readers but to that minority, the appeal is enormous. For instance, we get a lot of readers wanting to contact our birdwatching writer – either about something he has written or a bird they have spotted. It's hugely interesting to them and they value this outlet. It is a niche but it's a very important niche.

Debbie Hall, assistant publications editor with *Hull Daily Mail* publications, spends a lot of time producing these niche features, sometimes for the main paper, at other times for specialist supplements. A keen gardener and craftswoman, she enjoys the writing challenge of translating her passions into something that will inspire readers with the same enthusiasm.

> One of the nicest things I did was a Christmas supplement on how to do Christmas on a budget; basically showing readers how to make their own decorations and gifts – instructions on how to sew a felt gingerbread man, recipes, where mistletoe comes in ... the lot. I had to do a complete Blue Peter on it – step one, do this; step two ... and here's one I made earlier.
>
> We had a full Christmas team on it – we started in October and, I must admit, by mid-November I was all Christmas-ed out. It was really hard work but, at the same time, really enjoyable too because it was all my own ideas. It came straight from me. That was really rewarding.

Exercise

Write a travel feature based on your last holiday. Make sure you include a description of your destination and accommodation, travel information and price, as well as your impressions. Try to include a few anecdotes.

11 COMMISSIONING FEATURES

Don't be bashful ... nobody else will help you sell your copy – we freelances work alone and have to speak up for ourselves.

J. Dick, *Freelance Writing for Newspapers* (2003:43)

This chapter:

- examines how best to outline a feature idea
- looks at how to pitch or sell a feature
- considers the role of the commissioning editor.

When pitching a feature idea, one of the most important things to consider is whether or not what you are planning to write is suitable for the type of publication you are planning to write it for.

You might have a brilliant idea for a 2,000-word piece on ferret farming in South Wales but if the newspaper you are aiming it at carries features of no more than 800 words, is based in the North of England and has no interest in either South Wales or ferrets, then you are wasting your time. No matter how good the idea, no matter how much it interests *you*, and no matter how well written the feature, it will not be accepted if it is not suitable for the publication and its readership.

You must know your target market and, by that, we mean know and understand the type of features the newspaper generally carries. Ian Reeves, editor of the *Press Gazette*, the magazine for journalists, says if there is one rule, it is to make clear that you have read the newspaper or magazine you are pitching to. 'That blows everything else out of the water,' he says. 'The idea of pitching to a title that you aren't properly familiar with is crazy.'

> Susie Weldon, women's editor of the *Western Daily Press*, agrees:
>
> Nothing irritates me more than someone who hasn't done their homework – who knows nothing about the newspaper, its readership area and its style.
>
> When people approach me with feature proposals, I first look at the idea – is it interesting, have we already done it, and is it relevant to my readers? That's a mix of topic and geography – for example, we cover a large part of rural South West England and topics likely to appeal to rural women are of more interest to me than those aimed at inner-city women. But if they are aimed at women in North West England, then clearly I'm not interested.

Don't think you can buck the trend no matter how convinced you are that you have what it takes to enliven what you consider to be a staid newspaper with your innovative approach to journalism. If yours is a local paper that is heavily focused on community issues, the features editor is not going to entertain a piece about an obscure heavy metal rock band written in the idiosyncratic style of a heavy metal rock magazine.

Check that your idea is original, that it doesn't plagiarise anybody else's work and that it hasn't appeared already in the publication. Having done that, ask yourself: is it practical for me to research and write this piece? Can I get hold of the facts? Have I got access to the interviewees and have I the time to write the piece? Intriguing though it might be to write about the prime minister's views on salmon fishing in Scotland, access to him or her for an interview on this subject will be limited, if not denied, and interest among the readership of a local evening paper in, say, the Midlands, will be negligible.

If you are already working on a particular paper, you should know the type of features it carries because you will be – or should be – reading every issue. If you are a freelance, take the trouble to look through back issues of the paper you are targeting so see if what you are suggesting fits its style and content.

RIVETING STUFF ONLY, PLEASE

Ian Reeves objects to suggestions for ill-considered and fundamentally misjudged feature ideas:

> While I'm impressed that anybody can find 5,000 words to write on the captivating subject of 'the rivet crisis in lawnmower manufacturing', I'm afraid this is a magazine about journalism. Furthermore, the longest feature I ever run is 1,500 words. Obviously the journalist pitching the idea would have known these things if they had taken the trouble to read a copy of the magazine.

If you have an idea for a feature but are not sure where it would be best placed, have a look on the newsagent's shelves or check a media listings publication. There are dozens of special interest newspapers and magazines and one of them is bound to carry just the sort of subject you are planning to write about.

TARGET THE RIGHT PERSON

If you believe your idea is right for a particular newspaper, find the best person to send it to by ringing the newsdesk and asking who that would be. More than likely it will be the features editor, but it could also be another head of department. Prepare a summary and submit it to whoever it is that you have been advised is the most appropriate commissioning editor to approach.

As a staffer, you will probably simply tell the commissioning editor what the idea is about. If he or she is busy and asks you to send them an outline, keep it brief. Give a synopsis of the story in about three or four succinct paragraphs; say who you will be interviewing for the piece and why; and explain what the angle and/or peg is. Make sure the synopsis is fresh, interesting and well written – after all, this is something you are trying to sell so it should grab the feature editor's attention – and it should also indicate that you can string sentences together. If you are a freelance, do the same, but beware giving away too much information. It has been know for unscrupulous publications to steal an idea and give it to someone else to write.

> Ian Reeves warns against over-pitching:
>
> Don't send a pitch that itself is 800 words because you are giving away too much and wasting time.
> The art of writing a pitch – and it is an art – needs working on. It has to encapsulate the idea, the tone and the content of the piece in a captivating way that is going to hook the commissioning editor's attention. If you get that bit right, they then can be confident that you will be able to do the same for the reader. If you can penetrate the armoury of a cynical commissioning editor, there is a chance you can do the same for the reader.

As part of your freelance pitch, you should include some biographical details, for instance, explain who you are, the fact that you are a freelance journalist, and list some of the publications for which you have written in the past. Commissioning editors are busy people and are inundated with unsolicited ideas; they can only accept a tiny proportion of the submissions they receive. Why should they commission something from somebody they have never heard of on a subject that doesn't sound quite right?

TAKE A TIMECHECK

Timing your pitch is crucial, especially if you have a strongly time-sensitive peg. Susie Weldon says it is no good pitching a Valentine's Day feature to her on 10 February:

> My section comes out once a week so we've probably already covered Valentine's Day, unless 14 February falls on or just after my publication date and, in that case, I will already have planned what I'm going to do a good two weeks beforehand. On the other hand, it's no good pitching the Valentine's Day idea to me in June of the previous year – I don't work for one of the women's monthlies where they have long lead-in times. I can't deal with ideas that far in advance.

Pitching an idea to the right place at the right time is also important – and is often down to luck. Adam Wolstenholme, deputy news editor of the

Spenborough Guardian, succeeded in getting a freelance piece accepted by *The Times* at his first attempt. 'I'd had something on the back burner about smoking for some time. When National No Smoking Day was a few weeks away, I rang them. It obviously just fitted in with their plans – it was the timing that was everything.'

Since then, although he has had less success with *The Times*, he has had pieces accepted by *The Big Issue* and the *Leeds Guide*.

> Because it happened fairly easily first time around it gave me a false idea about how easy it was to keep doing it. I've tried things since without success. But you've got to be prepared to be knocked back a bit. You have to start from the premise that we all get kicked back and not take it personally.

SORRY, I DIDN'T CATCH YOUR NAME ...

Always be sure to get the commissioning editor's name right – and that means with the correct spelling and job title. A staffer should know these details and a freelance can find them by phoning the newspaper and asking, or by checking in the paper itself. Ian Reeves says he is not being egotistical when he insists that journalists get his name right: 'Buying the magazine will enable a freelance journalist to discover that my name is spelled with a double "e" and a "v" not a "d". And there's an "s" at the end.' If you get something like the commissioning editor's name wrong, how can anybody be sure that there are not other things wrong with your copy?

Check also whether you should e-mail, fax or post the idea.

> Jill Dick, author of *Freelance Writing for Newspapers*, advises sending a query letter first, followed by a telephone call. 'Random phone calls,' she says, 'can prove poor starters: the editor and his staff might just be extra busy when you call and your message could sit on an underling's desk as nothing more than a few scribbled words until the cleaners find it a week later. A similar fate may befall e-mailed copy or queries.' (Dick 2003: 42)
>
> Wolstenholme agrees that e-mail proposals can easily be ignored. Telephone calls, on the other hand, can be intimidating. 'But you've just got to bite the bullet and do it. It's a good idea to try and decide in advance the most newsy and original aspect of the piece you're offering.'
>
> Julie Gillin, who worked on the news desk at the *Sheffield Star* before turning freelance, says it helps that she has worked on the other side of the fence.
>
> *(Continued)*

> *(Continued)*
>
> I know how busy they are and that I've got just a short time to get them on board. However, because I know most of the journalists, it's not difficult approaching them about ideas but it can be quite nerve-wracking when you're talking to someone new.
>
> A key part of getting work accepted is knowing how the other person works. For instance, some computer systems don't allow journalists to open up attachments very easily so I send them stuff in the body of the e-mail. I also know that if I've got a story that would benefit from a picture to give them plenty of notice.
>
> The good thing is that over the years people have got to know my work and know that it will be decent.

A freelance should also remember not to confuse the names of different newspapers if they are sending the same feature idea to more than one outlet in the hope that one or the other will say yes. It has been known for a journalist to e-mail an idea to one newspaper or magazine, copy and paste it into an e-mail to a second and third but then forget to substitute the names of the second and third outlets for the original. While no commissioning editor will criticise you for trying to get published, they will take a dim view if you are touting the same idea to their competitors. Or, worse, they may feel they are being offered something that has been rejected elsewhere.

Says Julie Gillin: 'You must be organised and keep a proper record of who you have approached and with what.'

PATIENCE IS A VIRTUE – AND YOU'LL NEED TO CULTIVATE IT

A staffer will usually be told fairly quickly whether or not his or her feature idea works and if it is wanted. A freelance will more than likely have to chase up their original pitch either with a phone call or by e-mail. If this is the case, keep your enquiry light – avoid accusing the commissioning editor of ignoring you, and apologise for bothering them when they are obviously busy. Remind them of the peg if, for instance, the feature is tied to a date that is rapidly approaching. At this stage, the commissioning editor might ask you to send the original pitch again as they have mislaid it or not seen it. Don't worry and don't take it personally that your fabulous idea has been treated thus. Simply send the idea again and follow it up a couple of days later.

> You might be asked to send something in on spec – which means taking the time and trouble to research and write a feature and send it into the publication with no guarantee that it will be used. One woman's editor was renowned for saying 'Send it to me and I'll have a look', and then would sit on the piece without saying yes or no as the peg came and went, leaving the hapless writer in the dark despite the amount of work he or she had done. This attitude is lazy and rude but a sad fact of freelance life. Freelance writers have to learn to be patient yet persistent – and if they are having no success with one particular publication, they should look for another.
>
> In the past, it was known for freelance writers to offer the same feature idea to several different regional papers (so long as the piece was of general interest and not geographically specific – and so long as the circulation areas of the different publications did not overlap and they were not deemed to be in competition with each other). If one publication failed to use the feature, two or three others might. Given the poor rates of pay for regional features, sending the same feature to more than one regional newspaper was a way of making a decent amount of money per 1,000 words. Now a lot of the provincial regionals are owned by huge newspaper groups who like to have their own copyright deals and who issue contracts governing rights to freelance writers, which makes this former practice difficult. It is worth looking at the National Union of Journalists' booklet *Battling for Copyright* (NUJ 2004) for more information on this subject.

Even when a commissioning editor shows interest, they are likely to sit on the idea for some time and then, when all hope has died, contact you and ask for it immediately. So, having offered a suggestion for a feature, be sure you can get it written speedily.

YOU'VE SCORED!

Once an idea has been accepted, you should discuss how long the feature should be and what the deadline is. The commissioning editor might also have a view on the angle you should take or the way you should write the piece so that it fits in with something he or she might already be planning.

Most commissioning editors will brief a writer, discussing angles and possible interviewees. If you have been asked to write a feature, make sure you understand the brief and what is expected of you. Susie Weldon says it wastes her time if a writer doesn't stick to the brief:

Either I have to do quite a big editing job myself or send it back to them to re-write. If they've deviated too far, I may just reject the piece altogether. If, as a result of the interview or their research, they feel they have a better angle than the original, that is fine. But I would ask them to call me and discuss it first as there may be a reason why I want to go in on the original angle.

Having been asked to write, say, an 800-word feature, do not write 1,200. The commissioning editor will have a slot in mind for the piece and something that is over-written and cannot be subbed down quickly will risk being spiked. If you earnestly believe that the piece is worth more, try and persuade the commissioning editor. Discuss also your ideas for pictures and other illustrations that would go with the piece.

> Thinking ahead is crucial, says Julie Gillin:
>
> For instance, it's no good ringing the news desk at 10am and suggesting they send a photographer along because chances are they'll all be out covering a news story.
>
> Remember housekeeping issues too – like parking. Because I do a lot of health stuff, my photographs are often hospital-based where parking can be difficult, so I always make sure the photographer knows exactly where they can park so they don't waste 20 minutes driving around looking for a space.
>
> It's important too to keep people informed about what you're doing, especially if you've got something coming up in the future. Let the news desk know that you're working on something that you can't give them yet, but which might be useful to them later. It helps them with planning.

Once you have done your research and carried out the interviews, write the piece in a way that is appropriate to the subject and to the newspaper's own style.

Having been given a deadline, stick to it. Few things irk a commissioning editor more than having to chase up a writer and ask where the expected piece is. If your response is 'Oops. I've not started it yet', theirs will be to not use you again.

Save and keep copies of each feature you write in case the originals go missing or are accidentally wiped from the commissioning editor's PC.

Commissioning editors prefer writers who are hard-working, good-natured and uncomplaining. They do not like doing battle with writers who are precious about their work, so whatever you do, don't moan when an idea of yours is rejected or when your feature is cut by 500 words. Ask why, by all means, and treat the answer as constructive criticism or advice.

> Sid Langley, features editor at the *Birmingham Post*, says he is lucky in that he has a team of extremely talented writers: 'I only have to give them a brief and they get on with it. The problems come when I commission from a freelance writer who doesn't stick to the brief. It is no good producing a fairly soft feature when what I asked for was a hard political analysis, for instance.'
>
> He also commissions features via the news desk. For instance, if he wants a specialist feature on a major new road scheme in Birmingham, he will commission the transport correspondent to write the piece.

Jean Kingdon, editor of the *Ludlow Advertiser*, looks for readability, human interest, topicality, humour and good quotes in a feature:

> My staff know what I am looking for and will approach me with an idea for a feature. I know, obviously, how they work and think, and they know what will interest our readers. Because of that, I am willing to listen to any idea however outlandish. Recently our new trainee reporter did a couple of pieces having been on a balloon flight over Shropshire and a training stint in a glider.
>
> But in the main the *Advertiser*'s features are heavily community-based. We have run features on, for instance, the economic effects of a local town market closing, a close-up on our local secondary school, and a piece on a satirical band playing at a community centre.
>
> The *Advertiser*, like many local papers, doesn't have the budget for freelance writers generally and sometimes reviews and columns are written by readers who are often writing more for love than money.

As someone new to feature writing, you should keep cuttings of features you have had published and make a note of commissioning editors who have been particularly helpful and approachable. You will also need good contacts so keep your contacts book regularly updated.

WHERE SHOULD I SEND MY BILL?

A freelance writer should ask, once their feature idea has been commissioned, how much he or she will be paid – and when. If you are embarrassed about discussing money upfront, ask something like, 'Shall I invoice you or will I be paid automatically?' Whatever the answer, you can then follow up with, 'How much should I bill you for?' or 'How much should I expect?' or something similar. Do not expect to get paid until after publication of the feature – unfair but common practice – and expect that you may have to chase unpaid invoices until you are a regular contributor and registered on the publication's accounting system.

> Julie Gillin nurtures her relationship with the journalists on her patch. 'I keep in touch with them and e-mail them regularly, for instance, to congratulate them if they've had a good splash – they're the sort of little courtesies that keep any relationship happy. It also means that if I'm having trouble chasing payments, they'll help by chasing stuff at their end.'

As someone new to journalism, you might be tempted to write a freelance feature for nothing, simply to get into print. This is fine if you have the time and resources because (a) you are desperately keen to see your work in print and (b) how else are you going to start setting up a portfolio of your work? But we would hope you would not make a habit of it. Once you have had one or two features published and have proved you can do the job, you should insist on payment for any future work. If nothing else, writing articles for free sets an unhealthy precedent for those freelance journalists who have to make a living selling their work.

THANKS, BUT NO THANKS

Finally, don't take rejection personally. Ideas will fail for all sorts of reasons – the features editor has too much copy and not enough space; he or she is facing budget restrictions; he or she is having a bad day; the suggested peg doesn't work; or the idea is simply too obscure. Don't jettison the idea, re-work it or file it for future use – and try again later.

Ian Reeves says there are many factors involved in rejecting a feature:

> On a given week you might have three terrific pitches but which need to run at a specific time. We encourage features that are based on a news hook, so there are certain features which will only run one week and if you can't run them then, they will not run because they will lose the news edge. We only have a certain number of slots. Obviously, there are budgetary constraints too; we can only afford to commission so many features.

Nick Morrison, features editor of the *Northern Echo*, will reject features that don't fit the style of the newspaper, are not written well, or don't have a strong story. He also occasionally receives unsolicited features from people reminiscing about their childhood in the North East in a semi-fictional way:

We can't use them. People tend to think that if they consider something interesting or amusing, then everyone else will too. Some features are sent in by people from outside our circulation area so what they are writing about may have no geographical interest to the paper anyway – but some are sent in by readers and we don't want to lose them so we find a way of saying thanks, but no thanks.

Exercise

Select a feature from a regional daily newspaper. Imagine you are the writer but that it has not yet been published. Write a 100-word synopsis with which to sell the idea to a features editor.

12
WHY FEATURE WRITERS BECOME FEATURE WRITERS

You are the reader's ears, eyes and nose. Almost every day you meet people and see things that readers will never experience. If you don't tell them what these things are like, they will never know.

D. Randall, *The Universal Journalist* (2000: 182)

This concluding chapter:

- examines how – and why – the news journalist makes the transition from news to features

- looks at what motivates a reporter to move from the 'hard' world of news to the more 'liberated' style of features

- considers how a feature writer adapts and builds on valuable skills learned as a reporter.

Is it difficult to move from the hard-nosed, foot-in-the-door style of the news desk to the less highly charged atmosphere of the features department? Well, no. It's one of the most natural progressions there is. Many feature writers of our acquaintance started out in life as general news reporters and developed a love of writing that saw them move from the rough, tumble and ambulance-chasing of news to the depth, breadth and scope they saw in feature writing.

Julie Gillin, who now works as a freelance, muscled in on feature writing when she made the switch from the weekly *Derbyshire Times* to the evening *Sheffield Star*: 'I just really loved features and getting engaged with people in a way that you can't with news. And I like being able to write in my own style and develop my own ideas – being more descriptive and playing around with things.'

Not all feature writers though come from what might be called a conventional background. Freelance David Bocking, for instance, was a photographer whose NCTJ training included sessions on writing picture captions. 'I started with extended captions that gradually got longer and longer. Now I work as both a photographer and a writer. I still think I've got a lot to learn, especially about being more organised, but I enjoy the opportunity to find stuff out and meet people.'

> Martin Smith, writer in chief at the *Sheffield Star*, is another who took a circuitous route into features. He left school at 16 with next to no qualifications and spent 10 years as a sheet metal worker at Rolls-Royce before moving to Devon to work in a hotel kitchen. After 12 months in America and a further stint as a sheet metal worker, he did a degree at Trent Poly, now Nottingham Trent University, and an MA at Nottingham University, before joining the *Worksop Guardian*. After a spell at a news agency, he joined the *Sheffield Star* as a sub-editor. In the years since, he has worked as a news reporter and an action desk reporter, as well as chief reporter, assistant news editor and assistant sports editor. As writer in chief, his work is mostly feature-orientated:
>
> > As a writer, having a varied life experience helps – as a person I can see where people are coming from. It means I can empathise with them better and, hopefully, pick up on something interesting.
> >
> > There are a lot of things I like about features. I enjoy spending an hour talking to someone and then coming back and turning it into a double-page spread. It's the best thing – and the hardest thing. You're not just re-telling or describing, but shaping it and putting some of yourself into it. I like the fact that features allow you to add colour to a story and to express yourself in a way that you can't with news where you are just reporting what other people are doing.
> >
> > In a sense, I suppose I enjoy being able to craft pieces of writing that please me and, I hope, readers too.

It does not have to be a permanent one-way move though. Many news reporters write features as part of their daily work, developing a news story into a feature, taking a feature and turning it into a news story, writing a feature on their own specialist subject, or simply writing a general feature or news backgrounder following a brief from the news desk.

But separate camps do still exist: those reporters who prefer to stay in news and those who make the decision to move into features. David Charters of the *Liverpool Daily Post* did the latter, moving from a solid background in news to features:

> After three years on a twice-weekly local paper, I worked for a news agency serving national newspapers, before starting my own agency, which I ran for 16 years. The work I did for most of the time was news, though I had a yearning to do longer pieces and had several features published in the broadsheet papers.
>
> I have worked for the *Liverpool Daily Post* for 17 years, as a reporter and then as news editor, and for the past 7 years I have been a features and news-special writer. I have also written a weekly column for 15 years.
>
> There is nothing I dislike about writing features. I like them because of the people involved – most of them are endlessly fascinating.
>
> I always try to make my features interesting and try to write them well. Good writing is interesting in itself but with features you can be descriptive, tell jokes and make personal observations about your subject.

Chris Greenwood, now assistant news editor on the *York Evening Press*, was crime reporter, which meant he covered many of the paper's hardest news stories involving crimes, major incidents and court cases, but he relished the chance to write features too. He still works on day-to-day stories on tough subjects such as anti-social behaviour orders (ASBOs) and drink-related violence and he speaks to a number of different people to glean lots of information. But he adds: 'You can only put so much into a news story – a 40-word quote and the main points, for instance. It means you have a lot left that you haven't used, but you can put more of that into a feature – flesh out the detail behind the main news angle.'

Freelance journalist Lynne Greenwood says news was her first love, but after several years as a reporter on weekly, evening and two national daily papers, she made the shift in emphasis towards writing news features:

> If I was sent on a major news story as one of a team of reporters, I would often be asked to write an in-depth piece, a background feature or a profile interview of a major player in the story.
>
> By the time I chose to become a freelance writer, I enjoyed feature writing and knew that it offered more scope and possibilities than trying to compete with staff journalists and agencies on news coverage.

Greenwood likes building a piece from an original idea to a 1,000-word feature – and seeing it in print under a byline. But there are frustrations:

'I dislike the time it can take from start to finish, and it's annoying when I have talked to ten or more people and then discovered I only really needed three of them. It's also frustrating to see an idea which is still in your head, already in print – it means another writer got there first.'

During her career, Greenwood has worked on a wide variety of features:

> The most quirky has to be when I worked on a national tabloid and was sent to cover a *Guinness Book of Records* jamboree in Austria – attended by some of the most outrageous entries in the book. I will never forget watching Monsieur Mangetout eating a couple of cigarettes and then biting into the neck of a glass beer bottle – and chewing with relish.
>
> On a more serious note, it has been fascinating to meet some of the rich and famous in sport, theatre, television and public life, and one or two notorious people like the wife of the Yorkshire Ripper, Sonia Sutcliffe.
>
> But it is the features around people and families with unknown names, who are prepared to share their personal, often harrowing and moving experiences, which stay with me the longest.

Julie Gillin, who specialises in writing about health, says she has covered some breathtaking stories, including the first substantial interview with former England and Liverpool soccer player Emlyn Hughes shortly after he was diagnosed with cancer: 'Extracts from that piece were quoted again and again when he died', she says. Such interviews are memorable because of the celebrity of the person involved – others are simply too poignant to forget:

> One story that stands out was a piece I did about scalp cooling treatment. It's incredibly painful – patients wear a very cold cap, a bit like an old-fashioned swimming cap, that cools the head. The idea is that it helps prevent hair falling out after chemotherapy.
>
> I know losing hair is a very emotional thing but I couldn't understand why anyone would put themselves through this additional painful treatment until I talked to one woman, who didn't want to lose her hair because she hadn't told her family she was suffering from cancer.
>
> Her mother was very ill and she didn't want to add to the worry and stress for her family. Stories like that make you feel very, very privileged.
>
> Another one was a story about a little girl ice skater. She sent me a letter afterwards saying that she had loved the article and that she would still be reading it when she was granny. That was nice.

Anne Pickles, features editor of the *Yorkshire Evening Post*, was 12 years old when she realised journalism was for her – much to the disgust of her girls' grammar school headmistress:

She warned me that journalists were 'men who smoke and drink too much, wear shabby clothes and invade people's privacy'. Obviously, I wanted some of that.

I wanted to get behind the bald facts of news, help interpret the consequences of news events, bring home the impact every event had on our ordinary lives, and engage readers in much more than a quick headline hit. I wanted to be a stylish writer. I wanted to make a difference and be respected for it. I still do.

It was at the *Dewsbury Reporter* when I made my early forays into features and column writing – always about local people and local issues. I suppose it was there that I first realised it was possible to make a difference as a writer rather than a reporter. We regional journalists are always accountable for our actions and very contactable should anyone take issue with us. We can and do make a difference within our communities and to my mind that's what true journalism is – living where you work and understanding the people about whom you write.

BIBLIOGRAPHY

Bocking, D. (2005) 'Living with obsession', *Sheffield Telegraph*, 28 January.
Boulton, J. (2004) 'Boi, what a show', *Hull Daily Mail*, 15 October.
Bradshaw, P. (2005) 'Vera Drake', *Guardian,* 7 January.
Brockes, E. (2002) 'Jealous of Macaulay – are you kidding?', *Guardian*, 19 November.
Carter, H. (2001) 'The final whistle', *Guardian*, 24 October.
Clensy, D. (2004) 'Life after laughs', *Hull Daily Mail*, 16 October.
Culot, C. (2004) 'Beautiful actor who faced real life', *Eastern Daily Press*, 12 October.
Diamond, J. (1999) *C: Because cowards get cancer too*, London: Vermillion.
Dick, J. (2003) *Freelance Writing for Newspapers*, London: A&C Black.
Eastern Daily Press (2004) 'Mothers given hand to change their lives', 12 October.
Franklin, B. (1997) *Newszak and News Media*, London: Hodder Headline.
Gill, A.A. (2002) 'Table Talk: Fifteen', *Sunday Times Style,* 8 December.
Gill A.A. (2005) 'Table Talk: Pengelly's', *Sunday Times Style,* 20 March.
Glover, S. (ed.) (2000) *The Penguin Book of Journalism: Secrets of the press*, Harmondsworth: Penguin. (First published 1999 by Allen Lane.)
Greenstreet, R. (2003) 'Adam Duritz', *Guardian*, 15 February.
Greenwood, C. (2004) 'It's the trouble with guns', *York Evening Press*, 11 April.
Guardian (2005) 'Too many bills', 7 April.
Harcup, T. (2004) *Journalism Principles and Practice*, London: Sage.
Harding, L. (2001) 'In half a minute everyone was killed', *Guardian*, 29 January.
Hattenstone, S. (2004) 'Dame Judi, in brief', *Guardian*, 13 April.
Hennessy, B. (2003) *Writing Feature Articles*, London: Focal Press.
Hicks, W. (1999, repr.) *English for Journalists*, London: Routledge.
Hicks, W. with Adams, S. and Gilbert, H. (1999) *Writing for Journalists*, London: Routledge.
Hull Daily Mail (2004) 'King Bill rolls away on a high', 15 October.
Hull Daily Mail (2004) 'Life on the road is all the rage', 12 October.
Jones, J. (2000) 'How do you view?', *Guardian*, 19 October.
Jones, S. (2005) 'How I fought the travellers and won', *Daily Mail*, 4 March.
Lawrence, F. (2005) 'Polish workers lost in a strange land find work in UK does not pay', *Guardian*, 11 January 2005.
Marr, A. (2004) 'Between the lines', *Guardian*, 20 September.
McCabe, Cordoza M. (2000) *You Can Write a Column*, Cincinnati: Writers Digest Books.

McCabe, E. (2005) 'Nice try', *Guardian*, 7 April.
McNair, B. (2001, repr.) *News and Journalism in the UK*, London: Routledge.
Men's Health (2005) 'The better sex workout', May.
Millard, R. (2005) 'Debt juggling: the new middle-class addiction', *Sunday Times News Review*, 3 April.
NUJ (2004) *Battling for Copyright: Freelance journalists versus the media conglomerates*, London: National Union of Journalists.
Pape, S. and Featherstone, S. (2005) *Newspaper Journalism: An introduction*, London: Sage.
Parry, V. (2005) 'Last word: If it ain't broke, don't fix it', *Guardian*, 5 May.
Pax, S. (2004) 'Tigris Tales: If you want to stay alive, you had better obey the rules of the road – the road to and from Baghdad airport', *Guardian*, 21 April.
Randall, D. (2000) *The Universal Journalist*, London: Pluto Press.
Rayner, J. (1999) 'New school Thai', *Observer Magazine*, 5 September.
Rookes, L. (2005) 'Predictable wheeze', *Wakefield Express*, 13 May.
Sanders, K. (2004) *Ethics and Journalism*, London: Sage.
Sarler, C. (2000) 'Why tabloids are better', in S. Glover (ed.), *The Penguin Book of Journalism: Secrets of the press*, London: Allen Lane.
Stephenson, D. (1998) *How to Succeed in Newspaper Journalism*, London: Kogan Page.
Sunday Times (2004) 'A cockler's tale', 15 February.
Wakefield Express (2005) 'Queen's visit – latest', 4 March.
Wakefield Express (2005) 'Queen's coming to visit', 18 March.
Wakefield Express (2005) 'Day always marks the last supper', 25 March.
Wakefield Express (2005) 'Firm makes a mint', 25 March.
Wakefield Express (2005) 'Hand picked flower children', 25 March.
Wakefield Express (2005) 'It's a right royal occasion', 25 March.
Wakefield Express (2005) 'Queen handed warm welcome', 25 March.
Wakefield Express (2005) 'Maundy money on eBay', 6 May.
Walsh, G., Woods, R. and Sheridan, M. (2004) 'A cockler's tale', *Sunday Times*, 15 February.
Ward, L. (2005) 'Designer clothes, five properties – and £20,000 debt', *Guardian*, 5 April.
Weale, S. (2001) ' I Spy …', *Guardian*, 6 February.
Wheen, F. (2002) *Hoo-Hahs and Passing Frenzies: Collected journalism, 1991–2001*, London: Atlantic Books.

INDEX

accuracy, 33, 37, 38, 44–5, 115, 116
Adams, S., 57
advertising, 7
advertorials, 38, 90
age, 44–5
anecdotes, 49, 70–1, 87–8, 112
angles, 35, 43, 146
asides, 49
authoritative voice, 54, 112, 113

back-up columns, 100, 102
background features, 2, 6, 18, 80
Barber, L., 23, 25–6, 28, 34, 37, 83, 108
Barry, S., 129
Blunkett, D., 29
Bocking, D., 42, 46, 49, 59, 88, 152
body language, 28
book reviews, 117
Boulton, J., 68, 75
boxes, 50, 113–14
Bradley, M., 108
Bradshaw, P., 111–13
bridges *see* links
briefs, 145–7
broadsheet press, opinion in, 97
Brockes, E., 48
Burchill, J., 103
business features, 129

Carey, S., 45, 110
celebrity interviews, 27, 83–8
Charters, D., 26, 66, 88, 102, 153
checking information, 33, 37, 38, 44–5, 115, 116
Clensy, D., 67, 120
clothing, for interviews, 30
colour, 28, 51, 113
colour features, 80–1
columnists, 99–101
columns *see* niche columns; personal columns
commissioning editors, 141–4, 145–6
commissioning features *see* pitching feature ideas
conclusions *see* endings
conference calls, 32
conjunctions *see* links
consumer features *see* lifestyle features
contacts, 13, 126
    see also sources

contacts book, 18–22, 147
content, 5, 103, 110–14
context, in reviews, 111
control of interviews, 31
conversational interviews, 25–6
crime features, 18–19, 67, 129–33
criticism, in reviews, 113, 114, 119, 120
Culot, C., 67
cuttings, 16

deadlines, 3, 24, 64, 99–100, 146
Dench, Dame Judi, 84–7
Diamond, J., 103–5
Dick, J., 123, 139, 143
direct quotes, 46–7
doctors, 17, 125
documentaries, 117

e-mail interviews, 38–9
e-mailed pitches, 143, 144
editing
    by advertisers, 90
    by interviewees, 38
editorials *see* leader pages
editors *see* commissioning editors
education function, 5
endings, 61, 71, 74–5, 105, 128, 133
entertainment function, 5
events, as focus of features, 3
expert voice, 53–4, 128
    see also authoritative voice
expertise, in review writing, 110, 115
experts, as sources, 17

face-to-face interviews, 24–5, 28–9
facts, 44–5, 47, 67, 111, 113
fashionable language, 66
feature types, 6–8, 52, 80, 108
    advertorials, 38, 90
    colour pieces, 80–1
    follow-ups, 81–2
    leader pages, 6, 82
    news backgrounders, 2, 6, 18, 80
    personal columns *see* personal columns
    profiles, 7, 14, 34, 67, 83–8, 91
    reviews *see* reviews
    specialist *see* specialist features

feature writers, 5, 8–9, 124–5, 146–7, 152–5
feature writing
　getting started, 77
　see also writing skills; writing style
features
　based on news reports, 63
　commissioning see pitching feature ideas
　compared with news reports, 58–63
　nature of, 2–4
　news reports based on, 63
　prior viewing of, 38, 90
　relationship with news, 2
　role, 4–5
　structure see structure of features
　style see writing style
　time spent on, 64
film reviews, 111–13, 114–15
fine arts, 118
first impressions, 112
first-person style, 49, 92–3, 119
focus, 3–4
follow-up features, 81–2
food, writing about, 51, 118
Franklin, B., 7, 8
freebies, 89–90, 133–4
freelance writers, 124–5
　see also pitching feature ideas

general contacts, 21–2
general features, 6
genre, 5
Gill, A.A., 51, 68–9, 108
Gillin, J.
　on being a writer, 152, 154
　on commissioning features, 143–4, 146, 148
　on news vs. features, 59–60
　on sources, 17
　on specialist features, 125, 127, 134–5
Glover, S., 100, 101
gossip voice, 55
grammar, 46, 47
graphics, 49–50, 125
Greenstreet, R., 72
Greenwood, C., 18, 67, 129–32, 153
Greenwood, L., 13, 44, 59, 64, 153–4
Guiton, E., 89, 91, 96, 98, 99

Hall, D., 17, 137
Harcup, T., 65
Hattenstone, S., 84–7, 108
health features, 125–9
Hennessey, B., 41
Hicks, W., 72
honesty, 127
humour, 68–9, 104

imagery, 51, 70, 104, 113, 115
　in review writing, 113
images, 125
　see also graphics; pictures
indirect quotes, 47
information, 44–5, 47, 111, 113
information box/panel, 50, 113–14
information function, 4
interest, 3–4
　see also local interest
interview questions, 34–6
　prior viewing of, 37–8
interviewees
　encouraging, 36
　prior viewing of article, 38
　prior viewing of questions, 37–8
　relationship with, 27–8, 31
　researching, 26
　see also quotes
interviews
　with celebrities, 27, 83–8
　control of, 31
　dress for, 30
　by e-mail, 38–9
　ending, 37
　face-to-face, 24–5, 28–9
　introductions, 30, 45
　length, 27, 34
　location, 28–30
　news vs. features, 24–5
　and photographers, 31–2
　preparation, 25–6, 33
　professional behaviour, 30, 36–7
　punctuality, 30, 84–7
　setting up, 27–8
　by telephone, 24, 32–3, 84–7
　tools for, 33–4
　and writing style, 91–2
introductions, 35, 67–9
　building on, 69–70
　in interviews, 30, 45
　news vs. features, 60–1
　to crime features, 133
　to personal columns, 103
　to reviews, 119
issues, as focus of features, 3

Jacobson, H., 103
jobs section, as source, 13–14
Jones, J., 118
Jones, S., 68

Kelner, M., 91, 101–2
Kingdon, J., 3–4, 147
KISS and tell principle, 58
knowledgeable friend voice, 54–5

INDEX

Lahive, K., 127, 128–9
Langley, S., 6, 8, 147
language
    linking words and phrases, 44, 71–4
    in reviews, 111, 113
    tense, 62, 75–6, 116, 117
    use of, 66
    use of 'said', 76
    voice, 53–5
    see also writing style
Lawrence, F., 3
leader pages, 6, 82
length of features, 3, 6, 59–60, 76–7
    concise writing, 58, 99
    cutting, 14, 77
    reviews, 109
    sticking to brief, 146
length of interviews, 27, 34
letters, pitching via, 143
lifestyle features, 7–8, 135–6
links, 44, 71–4
local interest, 3–4, 50–1, 133, 140
location of interviews, 28–30

McCabe, E., 54
McCabe Cardoza, M., 95
McNair, B., 7–8
Marr, A., 5
medical approach to health features, 126
middles, of features, 61, 70–1, 104–5, 133
Millard, R., 63
Morrison, N., 2, 124, 136, 148–9
multiple questions, 35
music reviews, 110, 114, 115, 118

names, spelling, 44
narrative style, 67, 69–70
news, relationship with features, 2
news in brief (NIB), 13, 60, 112
news interviews, 24
news reporters, 152, 153
news reports
    based on features, 63
    compared with features, 58–63
    features based on, 63
    follow-up features, 81–2
    see also background features
newspapers
    opinion pieces, 97
    as sources, 13–14, 16
    style of, 52
    suitability of article for, 140–1
NIB (news in brief), 13, 60, 112
niche columns, 136–7
note-taking, 33–4

objectivity, 59
off-diary sources, 14–16
on-diary sources, 15, 16
opinion, 48–9
    leader pages, 6, 82
    reviews, 113, 114, 118–19
    see also personal columns
opinion pieces, 96–7
organization contacts, 19–20
originality, 140

panels, 50, 113–14
Parry, V., 126
partial quotes, 47
past tense, 62, 75–6, 116
patience, 144–5
Pax, S., 48, 49
payment, 147–8
Peel, J., 107
pegs, 27, 42–3, 60
people, as focus of features, 3
people contacts, 20–1
perks *see* freebies
personal columnists, 96, 99–101
personal columns, 108
    back-up columns, 100, 102
    ideas for, 101–2
    nature of, 8, 89, 96–8
    purpose of, 101
    rules for writing, 103–5
    style and content, 98–9, 103
    USP of, 98, 101
personal details, 44–5
personal pronouns, 49, 92–3, 119
personality, 59
persuasion function, 5
photographers, 31–2, 49–50, 146
Pickles, A., 12, 24, 25, 28, 58, 154–5
pictures, 32, 49–50, 125, 132, 146
pitching feature ideas
    acceptance and briefs, 145–7
    following-up, 144–5
    means of, 143–4
    payment, 147–8
    rejection, 148–9
    suitability for publications, 140–1
    target person, 141–2
    timing, 142–3
plays *see* theatre reviews
preconceptions, in review writing, 111–12
present tense, 62, 75–6, 116, 117
press releases, 15, 83
preview features, 81
professional behaviour, 30, 36–7
profiles, 7, 14, 34, 67, 83–8, 91
psychological approach to health features, 126

public, as sources, 17
public relations officers (PROs), 27, 32, 83
punctuality, 30, 84–7
purpose, 4, 101, 119

Q&A style, 91–2
quality, 6
quantity *see* length of features
questions, 34–6
   in intros, 68
   prior viewing of, 37–8
quotes, 14, 45–7
   news vs. features, 61
   in reviews, 113, 117
   use of 'said', 76
   within structure, 68, 70–1

radio reviews, 116–17
Randall, D., 96, 151
readers
   journalist as delegate of, 25
   referred to as 'you', 93, 105
   writing for, 3–4, 42–3, 100, 109
Reeves, I.
   on nature of features, 4, 6, 66
   on pitching ideas, 140, 141, 142, 148
   on rules for writing, 59
regional newspapers, pitching to, 140, 145
regular niche columns, 136–7
regular sources, 16–17
rejection, 148–9
research, 6, 14, 26
restaurant reviews, 51, 118
reviews, 89–90, 108
   book, 117
   content, 110–14
   expertise, 110, 115
   film, 111–13, 114–15
   fine arts, 118
   music, 110, 114, 115, 118
   opinion, 113, 114, 118–19
   purpose, 119
   restaurant, 51, 118
   rules for, 109–10, 119–20
   television and radio, 116–17
   tense, 76
   theatre, 114, 115, 116
Richardson, C., 13
Rookes, L., 54–5
rules
   news vs. features, 59–60
   for personal columns, 103–5
   for reviews, 109–10, 119–20

Sanders, K., 11
Sarler, C., 99
shorthand, 33–4

sidebars, 50
Smith, M., 27, 29, 31, 152
soap reviews, 117
sources, 3, 43
   contacts book, 18–22, 147
   off-diary, 14–16
   on-diary, 15, 16
   regular, 16–17
   relationship with, 17, 130
   selecting, 12–14
   see also contacts; interviewees
special interest subjects, 7
specialisation, 108
specialist features, 6–7, 88, 124–5
   business, 129
   crime, 18–19, 67, 129–33
   health, 125–9
   regular niche columns, 136–7
   travel, 133–5
   women's/lifestyle, 7–8, 135–6
specialist sources, 17, 18
specialist writers, 124
spelling, 33, 37, 44, 115, 116
star-ratings, 110, 114
statements of fact, 47, 67
Stephenson, D., 1, 2, 3, 79, 82, 97, 98
structure of features, 66–71
   crime features, 133
   endings, 61, 71, 74–5, 105, 128, 133
   health features, 128–9
   introductions, 35, 60–1, 67–9, 103, 119, 133
   links, 44, 71–4
   middles, 61, 70–1, 104–5, 133
   personal columns, 103–5
   reviews, 119
style *see* feature types; writing style
subjects *see* interviewees
synopses, 141–2

tabloid press, opinion in, 97
tape recorders, 33
telephone interviews, 24, 32–3, 84–7
telephone pitches, 143
television reviews, 116–17
tense, 62, 75–6, 116, 117
theatre reviews, 114, 115, 116
themes, 74–5
time spent on features, 64
timing
   of pitch, 142–3
   see also deadlines
tone, 52–3
topicality, 50, 133
transition phrases *see* links
travel features, 133–5

USP (unique selling point), 98, 101

voice, 53–5, 112, 113, 116, 128

Ward, D., 17
Weale, S., 68
Weldon, S., 6, 13, 136, 140, 142, 145–6
Williams, Z., 99, 100, 108
Wolstenholme, A.
  on features vs. news, 48, 58
  on interviews, 30
  on personal columns, 96, 100, 101, 102
  on pitching ideas, 142–3
  on reviews, 109–10, 114–15, 119

women's features, 7–8, 135–6
word length *see* length of features
writers *see* feature writers
writing skills, 6, 42, 66
  colour, style and tone, 51–3
  concise writing, 58, 99
  links, 44, 71–4
  voice, 53–5
writing style, 52, 90–1
  first-person, 49, 92–3, 119
  in lifestyle features, 135, 136
  narrative, 67, 69–70
  news vs. features, 58
  Q&A, 91–2